You Can Coach

How to Help Leaders Build Healthy Churches through Coaching

Joel Comiskey
Sam Scaggs
Ben Wong

 CCS Publishing

www.joelcomiskeygroup.com

Published by CCS Publishing
23890 Brittlebush Circle
Moreno Valley, CA 92557 USA
1-888-344-CELL

Cover design by Josh Talbot
Lay-out by Sarah Comiskey
Editing by Scott Boren
Copy editing by Susan Osborn

LCCN: 2010920027

ISBN: 978-0-9843110-4-0

CCS Publishing is the book-publishing division of Joel Comiskey Group, a resource and coaching ministry dedicated to equipping leaders for cell-based ministry.

Find us on the World Wide Web at **www.joelcomiskeygroup.com**

Praise for *You Can Coach*

As the cell church movement has matured, every nation on the earth has discovered the need for Kingdom Coaching. While many secular writers have published in this field, this book is for those of us who have been called by God to form two-winged bodies of Christ.

It is most significant that this book demonstrates our theology of community, critical to all cell principles. It is the work, not of one author, but a community of three – all seasoned veterans within the movement. Experienced, indeed! I would estimate the total years these men have invested in developing cell groups is more than 60 years! From Asia, from South America, from the U.S., have come insights crafted by men who are practitioners, not theoreticians.

Their chapters reflect not human principles but rather Kingdom principles. They have performed well in all parts of the earth as these men have coached. That is extremely important. Other treatments of this subject may reflect only cognitive, affective, and psychomotor domains; these chapters also include the Christ-directed domain.

Reader, prayerfully ask not only, "Who shall I coach?" but also pray, "Who will I prepare to coach using this material?" We need a rapid development of coaches for the ever growing harvest. This is the tool to use!
— **Dr. Ralph W. Neighbour, Jr.** Adjunct Professor of Cell Church Ministries, Golden Gate Theological Seminary

"Here is a compelling case for coaching from three world-class coaches who are gifted at releasing extraordinary coaching in anyone who wants the best for the people they serve. After over a decade of training coaches world-wide, I am thrilled that this book is now in your hands and soon in your heart. It simplifies and condenses the power of the coaching process and will multiply your confidence and competence as a coach and leader."
— **Dr. Joseph Umidi** Founder & President of Lifeforming Leadership Coaching, www.lifeformingcoach.com

Coaching is not just for sports! My high school coach was probably the most influential teacher in my life, and his ability to draw us out as students was at the heart of our school's ability to create great teams. What clearly comes out in this great introduction to coaching by Joel Comiskey and team is that coaching is for life, particularly for church life and leadership development. Jesus is our model, and His passion for working with His disciples is mirrored in this excellent account from well-known cell church leaders. Every church leader will benefit from the lessons and examples provided in this book.
— **Tony and Felicity Dale** authors of *The Rabbit and The Elephant* and well-known pioneers within house church movements world-wide

If you are the type of person who wants to help other people be successful, then this book is for you. Joel, Sam, and Ben are 3 people who have found that coaching plays a major role in assisting people fulfil their destiny in life. Three coaches, three differing approaches, one passion: To serve other people for their success. Here is a wealth of information and personal insights that will give you the tools and the courage to believe that you too can coach others into their best possible future.

— **Michael Mackerell** Author, Stadia East Regional Director, professor, and veteran church planter

You Can Coach is an excellent read on the intentional encouragement of local church leaders from three experienced coaches of coaches. However, the principles unpacked here contain valuable insights for general mentoring. The three perspectives of the authors encourage a healthy comparative analysis. They also illustrate that good mentoring needs to be contextualized and doesn't have to look the same. I plan to make this book a high priority read for our ministry team and for those I coach!

— **Bob Moffitt** President of the Harvest Foundation and author of *If Jesus Were Mayor*

Someone has said, "The era of seminars will soon come to an end; but the era of coaching has come of age."

This is a must-read book for every coach, pastor and cell leader. It is full of helpful insights and practical ideas, and is also easy to read. Readers will be motivated to coach, and will find the principles and methods outlined very useful in their coaching.

— **Tony Chan** Co-founding Pastor of Shepherd Community Church, Hong Kong

"It is lonely at the top!" Every pastor or marketplace leader needs someone to walk with them, dream with them, listen to them, ask the hard questions, and share their burdens. In short, leaders long for a coach. If you have a heart to be coach, this book will get you started. Wong, Comiskey and Scaggs have been coaching for years and have a desire to multiply the ranks of people who will coach. Come journey with them. You too can coach!

— **Darrow L. Miller** Author and Co-Founder of Disciple Nations Alliance

Praise for *You Can Coach*

For the last 20 years of ministry as a missionary, pastor, church planter, entrepreneur and mentor I have focused my work on 2 Timothy 2:2: "And the things you have heard me say in the presence of many witnesses, entrust to reliable men who will also be qualified to teach others." In "You Can Coach" Sam, Ben and Joel have reinforced the mandate that each of us need a Paul and a Timothy with which to go through life. If God is calling you to invest in the lives of others this book is a must read. Each of their unique perspectives and life experiences work together in the book to help clarify what a coach is, how to best learn from others, and explore several different models of coaching that can be easily put into practice. Surely this timely message will be used across the globe to inspire, equip, and encourage many who are serving in the Lord's harvest. On a personal level, I am grateful for the friendship and wisdom Sam, Ben, and Joel have offered me over the years. I am looking forward to using the principles from You Can Coach with those leaders the Lord brings my way.

— **Eric Watt** Sr. Pastor of Greenbrier Church, Chesapeake, VA and the Founder and President of Reaching Unreached Nations and the Founder and CEO of, MPOWR, LLC.

For several years I have been involved in coaching pastors and leaders and was greatly encouraged as I read this book. I recommend this book for the following people: Those who think that coaching is just a temporary trend; those who have attended every kind of seminar, but who still realize that they are in a lonely battle for cell ministry; and especially for those who want to get down there with the struggling pastors and leaders and help make a difference.

— **Eiichi Hamasaki** JCMN Coaching Network Coordinator and pastor of Otsu Baptist Church in Japan

"This book is full of faith in the reader, and every page is eager to send the message that "you can coach!" The three different authorotative voices follow the same thread, and allow for different paths toward the same goal. I highly recommend this timely book."

— **Øystein Gjerme** Pastor of Bergen City Church, Norway

Praise for *You Can Coach*

As a professional coach, I've read many books about coaching with more or less happiness. Something was lacking until "You can coach". This "Teambook" is an awesome tool for every Christian dreaming to be empowered for reaching the next level of efficiency in life, relationships, and ministry. A "Must Have". The art of Coaching is presented from a real and authentic perspective that will give you transposing core values of coaching to apply in your own experience. In this book, you'll find a clear and Kingdom oriented frame and basic principles which the church needs at the beginning of this century. Finally, you'll get concrete tools that will lead you on the way of a coaching lifestyle because... You can coach!

— **Jean-Marc Terrel** Entrepreneur and Coach Trainer in France

Everyone needs a coach. You will be lonely and limited if you don't have one. Everyone can be a coach, and as you coach, you grow in many ways out of your expectation. This book is a such a powerful and practical guide for coaching. The coaches writing this book are not just scholars, knowing and sharing some principles. They are practical and fruitful coaches sharing biblical and workable keys from their daily experience. Read this book and start doing it tomorrow. Yes, you can coach.

— **Sunny Cheng** Coordinator of the Hong Kong Cell Church Network

This is a coaching classic! Having three contributors provides a broad spectrum of insights and concepts on this vital subject and removes "the óne size fits all" approach. The vast experience of the authors is revealed in an easy to understand format, making successful coaching an attainable goal for anyone and everyone.

— **Stuart Gramenz** Author, pastor, and coach

My friends Joel Comiskey, Sam Scaggs, and Ben Wong have given us an exceptional resource to advance the Kingdom of God. Their new book *You Can Coach: How to Help Leaders Build Healthy Churches through Coaching* is clearly biblical, very practical, and a refreshing read. If you are really serious about growing as a Christian leader, this book is for you. I highly recommend this book to every present and aspiring Christian leader who desires to make his or her life count for the Kingdom of God. Thank you Joel, Sam, and Ben, for giving us this outstanding book. You are living what you have written.

— **Larry Kreider** Author and International Director of DOVE International

Praise for *You Can Coach*

The Kingdom of God describes healthy growth typically in three stages as in stalk, head, kernel or child, man, father. To assist people in Kingdom growth, everyone needs spiritual parenting - and then move on to parent others. Joel, Sam, and Ben have pooled their long years of coaching experience and created a very helpful and motivating introduction to the lost art of creating a safe place for people - and entire churches! - to be coached and therefore practically launched into their Kingdom destiny.

— **Wolfgang Simson** Author of "The Starfish manifesto"

Experiential, practical, and technical. All in one. A masterpiece in its own rights, this book sheds light on the topic of coaching, convincing the reader to embark on this wonderful journey of helping to mature and grow the Body of Christ. You can do it! Just do it! I highly recommend it for your reading and practicing.

— **Robert Michael Lay** Founder and president of Cell Church Ministries in Brazil (this ministry also trained thousand of pastors in South America)

Regarding my faith journey, I couldn't remember if there was one specific coach who ever helped me in my Christian walk until I met Ben Wong, the Pastor of Shepherd Community Grace Church in Hong Kong. He spent a lot of time with me, mostly on very close, personal Coaching. And the contents of his coaching may surprise you – we often ate together, joking, and having fun together. We would talk about our family, and he would also share many of his thoughts and feelings on doing ministry. Of course, he would also be concerned about my ministries. We often chatted until late into the night before going to bed. He often took initiative to approach people, and I was so touched by his sincere attitude, which made me feel accepted and highly valued.

He has helped me with his full-strength and never turned down my requests. He has been doing his best to meet my needs. During the past few years, he came to Taiwan several dozen times to help us out. He has brought significant impacts on myself and on the church where I serve. He has widened my perspectives toward the Kingdom of God and the biblical worldview, and he has influenced me deeply on doing church networking, missions, and some other important perspectives and issues like the holistic ministries. What he has done in Shepherd Community Grace Church, CCN-Hong Kong, and churches in Japan consistently demonstrate his church perspectives, which he gleaned from the Holy Bible. Through the experiences I learned from his personal coaching and helping, I try to apply them to my church and to the ministries of Taichung Strategic Alliance."

His sincere attitude towards his family and family members also influenced me deeply. As a result, over these years, my marriage and relationships with my two daughters have been improved.

Because I have benefited from personal coaching greatly, I hope you may have opportunity to receive the benefits of coaching and may become other people's coach as well.

The book "You Can Coach" which I would greatly recommend, is a practical handbook, which can help us becoming a more effective coach. The future church needs a lot of coaches who are willing to be other people's spiritual parents. I believe this book can help you out with this purpose.

— **Timothy Tu** Senior Pastor of Taichung Grace Church

Table of Contents

Praises 3

Acknowledgements 13

Introduction 15

  A Trio of Coaches 16

  Differences in our Coaching Strategies 18

  Learning to Coach 19

Chapter 1 : Everyone Needs a Coach by Ben Wong 21

  Coaching in Life 22

  Coaching Disciples 23

  Coaching as a Pastor 23

  Pastors Need Coaching 24

  Building an Exemplary Church 26

  My Church is Your Church 27

  My Journey into Coaching Other Pastors 27

  Coaching Group 28

  We Need More Coaches! 29

Chapter 2: Dream-based Coaching by Sammy Ray Scaggs 31

  What Is Coaching? 34

  Basic Disciplines of Coaching 35

    1. Know Yourself 35

    2. Active Listening 37

    3. Ask Powerful Questions 39

    4. Positive Affirmation 42

  Examples of Dream-based Coaching 44

  Where Do You Go from Here? 47

Chapter 3: The Coaching Toolbox by Joel Comiskey 49

  Learning from Feedback 50

Table of Contents

Using Everything in the Toolbox 50

Variety of Leaders and Situations 51

Get to Know the Leader 53

Bedrock Foundation of Coaching 54

Following the Spirit of God 54

Coaching Is an Art 55

Freely Giving to Others 55

A Few Steps Ahead 57

Evaluating What Works 58

Chapter 4: Principles We Have Learned in Coaching 59
by Ben Wong

Coaching is Serving – Not Controlling 59

Coaching Is about the Whole Person 61

Coaching Is a Priority 64

Coaching Is Relationship 65

Coaching Is Encouraging 66

Coaching Is Drawing on Many Resources 68

Coaching Is Helping the Person to Trust God 68

Coaching is Church to Church 69

Coaching Is Helping Pastors of Small Churches 70

Chapter 5: Friendship-based Coaching by Joel Comiskey 73

Sharing the Journey 73

Relational Authority that Comes from Friendship 75

More than Results 76

Ebbs and Flows 77

Confidentiality 77

Practical Suggestions 79

Everyone Can be a Friend 79

Chapter 6: Ordinary Pastors Can Coach by Ben Wong 81

People Helpers 82

Coaching Networks 83

Hong Kong Coaching Network 88

Coaching Must Produce Coaches 89

We Can Do It! 91

Chapter 7: The Most Common Pitfalls of Coaching 93
by Sammy Ray Scaggs

Pitfall #1: Not Having the Heart of a Coach 95

Pitfall #2: Seeing the Person You Are Coaching 97
with Limited Vision 70

Pitfall #3: Being a Dream Killer Rather Than a 99
Dream Releaser

Pitfall #4: Not Listening but "Telling" the Coachee 101
What to Do

Pitfall #5: Trying to Do Something that Has Never 102
Been Done for You

Pitfall #6: Coaching for Fun, Fad or Fascination 103

Chapter 8: Coaching by Focusing on the Essence 107
by Ben Wong

Seven Essences of the Church 108

Why We Need Coaches 109

Essence 1 – Relationship 111

Essence 2 – Participation 114

Essence 3 – Empowering 117

Essence 4 – Focusing on Jesus 120

Essence 5 – Outreach and Multiplication 122

Essence 6 – Networking 124

Essence 7 – Adaptable Structures 126

Conclusion 127

Chapter 9: Making a Coaching Plan by Joel Comiskey 129

Make a Plan and be Ready to Adjust 129

1. Begin with a foundation of knowledge 130

2. Build a Case Study of Pastor and Church 131

Who the Pastor Is 132

History and Background of the Church 132

The Community and Cultural Context 132

Attempts at Cell Ministry 132

3. Develop a Concrete Church Action Plan 133

Table of Contents

Transitioning	133
Planting	134
Training Track and Care System	135
Budget	135
Faith Goals for New Cell Groups	135
4. Fulfill the Action Plan: On-going Coaching	136
5. Coaching someone else	137
You Can Coach	138
Appendix 1: Comiskey's Coaching Evaluation	139
Oral/Personal Evaluation	139
Anonymous Evaluation	139
The Form I Use for the Anonymous Evaluations	140
Appendix 2:Ben Wong's Coaching Agreement	143
Basic Proposals	144
Index	147
Endnotes	151

Acknowledgements

In the long process to make this book a reality, many hands and eyes have handled and contributed to the final work. Several people deserve special recognition.

Bill Joukhadar spent a huge amount of volunteer time to correct numerous grammatical in the initial draft. His diligent effort made this book much cleaner and easier to read.

Special thanks to Linda Johnson, an English teacher, who volunteered her English expertise to pinpoint errors and help the final work flow much better.

We're grateful to Brian McLemore, World Bible Translation Center's (www.wbtc.org) Vice President of Translations, who critiqued this book, and the result is a better book.

We appreciated Jay Stanwood's wise, common sense advice on how to reword obscure phrases. Jay helped us rephrase sentences and rethink difficult concepts. Rae Holt took his time to read the manuscript, point out difficult phrases, and offer important encouragement.

Rob Campbell, Steve Cordle, and Jeff Tunnell offered timely advice to make the final manuscript much better. We really appreciated the time they took to look over this book.

We're grateful for Susan Osborn's skill in copyediting the final edition of this book. Scott Boren, our chief editor, continues to do an incredible editing job.

Introduction

John Wooden died on June 04, 2010. His ten national championships at UCLA (University of California in Los Angeles) over a 12-year period are unmatched by any other college basketball coach. He also guided UCLA to eighty-eight consecutive victories and seven straight national championships. No other coach has matched such a feat.

How did John Wooden become such a great coach? For one thing, Wooden lived the life he hoped others would follow. Wooden himself was a great basketball player and was inducted to the Hall of Fame as a player. The principles he applied to his own life were later used in his coaching. He practiced what he preached, and others were inspired to follow.

John Wooden coached players to become better people on and off the court, which translated into better basketball players. Wooden developed the total character of each player to succeed in sports and life. He imparted life lessons far more enduring than an offensive play or how to make a hook shot. After retiring from basketball, business organizations asked Wooden to lecture and share his timeless principles, and he willingly did so.

Wooden developed pithy sayings to develop character, such as:
- "What you are as a person is far more important than what you are as a basketball player."
- "You can't live a perfect day without doing something for someone who will never be able to repay you."
- "Success is never final; failure is never fatal. It's courage that counts."

We've entitled this book *You Can Coach* because we believe that coaching is more about passing on tested life principles, rather than formal techniques. One who has the heart of a coach believes in people and their dreams to live the life they were meant to live. A coach values one-on-one relationships and comes alongside the individual to help him or her release their potential and then to hold the person accountable to accomplish their dreams.

Today we are inundated with books and seminars (information), but many pastors are not equipped to apply that knowledge. They need a coach. They need someone who will listen, encourage, and challenge them to take the next step. Someone who will model real leadership for them.

A Trio of Coaches

At the 2008 Cell Church Mission Network gathering in Hong Kong, Ben Wong asked various coaches to share why coaching was so important to them. We heard coaches from Japan, Korea, Hong Kong, Taiwan, and North America talk about their coaching networks. We broke up into sub-groups to talk about coaching and how to implement it.

Then Ben Wong asked those interested in coaching to meet with him in California in June 2009. Various ones met, and three of those attendees joined together to write the book you now hold in your hands. We wanted it to be a coaching book, written by authors who are practicing coaching.

We also wanted to write a book from a global coaching perspective, so in this book you'll learn about coaching as practiced in various parts of the world including, China, Japan, Taiwan, and North America.

Joel Comiskey is now in his tenth year of coaching pastors since connecting with those first pastors in 2001. Most of his learning was gained from being in the battle. His three chapters in this book are the fruit of what he's learned while coaching, reflecting, adapting, and then continuing the process. He has written two books on coaching: *How to be a Great Cell Group Coach* (Touch 2004) and *Coach*

(CCS Publishing, 2008). Joel is founder of Joel Comiskey Group, a ministry dedicated to resourcing the worldwide cell church movement, and Joel also teaches as an adjunct professor at several theological seminaries. Joel and his wife, Celyce, have three daughters and live in Moreno Valley, California.

Sammy Ray Scaggs is a pastor, teacher, author, and missionary. He has planted churches in his home country, the United States, as well as in Italy and Albania. He has a heart for cross-cultural and international ministry. He has written a new book called *The DreamWeaver* (Xulon Press). Sam is an integral part of a worldwide coaching network called Transformational Leadership Coaching, serving as the Vice President and International Director. The content of his two chapters in this book, *You Can Coach*, is rooted in his practical hands-on coaching and global coach training experience. Sam Scaggs has always been passionate about coaching. He has been coaching pastors and leaders for over twenty years. He's also the co-founder of an organization called Equity-forming Financial Coaching, which combines the expertise of sound biblical financial principles with the power of coaching. Sam resides in Virginia with his wife of thirty-four years, and they have two married daughters and two grandsons.

Ben Wong has been coaching pastors and leaders for fifteen years. He has written four chapters in this book, and you'll discover that Ben believes anyone can be an effective coach. He has also written the book, *Making a Permanent Difference: Investing your life in Others* (Touch Limited International). Ben has been instrumental in starting a coaching movement in Asia and South America. Ben has the heart of a coach, and it is evident from the first time you sit down to talk with him. He has experienced the triumphs and difficulties of ministry, and he is ready to listen to people and ask questions. Ben has the ability to discern what is in the heart of a leader and coach them to higher levels. He has been coaching leaders from many parts of the world and has been used of the Lord to not only plant a thriving cell church in Hong Kong but also to launch the

Cell Church Missions Network with hundreds of leaders networking together to strengthen national churches and working together to plant churches among some of the least reached peoples on the planet. Cynthia, Ben's wife, helps him in coaching and they have three grown children.

Differences in our Coaching Strategies

While we as authors/coaches agree on most points, you'll also notice some distinct differences.

Sam Scaggs, for example, believes that coaches should not start with giving advice, teaching or offering counsel when launching a coaching relationship. While agreeing that those "tools" are always needed, his style is to begin with asking key questions. One of the roles of the coach, according to Sam, is to draw out the God-given dream inside the one being coached through the process of asking powerful questions, then to move on to using teaching, training, resources, and other tools as the coaching relationship develops.

Joel Comiskey, on the other hand, writes about using everything in the toolbox, including listening, asking powerful questions, counseling, and teaching, if it serves the coachee (a term used throughout this book to refer to the one being coached) and makes him a better leader.

You'll also notice that some of us request a fee for coaching, while others do not. Both are acceptable. Ben Wong views coaching as volunteer ministry. Ben receives financial support from the church he founded, Shepherd Community Church, in Hong Kong. Thus, when he travels around the world to coach pastors and start coaching movements, he does this voluntarily. He expects those in his network also to coach others free of charge. On the other hand, Sam Scaggs and Joel Comiskey both charge a fee for coaching. Sam does 50% of his coaching as a volunteer with pastors and charges a fee to coach executives in the business world. For both Sam and Joel, coaching is a means of supporting their families.

While both Sam and Joel do participate in a limited amount of free coaching, their desire is to get to the point where all coaching could be accomplished without request for compensation. Please keep these differences in mind when reading the different chapters of this book.

One unique aspect of this book is the idea that churches can also coach other churches. An entire church might feel a burden to help another church and then use the principles found in this book to coach that church.

Learning to Coach

In this book, you'll learn to become an effective coach by understanding:

- Why coaching is so important.
- Coaching principles that apply in every culture.
- How to dream for your coachee.
- How to use all the coaching tools in your toolbox.
- How to make a coaching plan.
- How to evaluate your coaching.

We don't believe that coaching should be left in the hands of professionals only. You don't need a higher level degree to coach someone else. You learn the most by doing it, reflecting on your coaching, and then evaluating what works. Coaching is best caught rather than taught.

It is our passion that every pastor and leader who reads this book will be encouraged to embrace the heart of a coach and help to release the dreams and potential of those God has placed in their sphere of influence. Remember, You Can Coach. Take that step of faith to become God's instrument to add value to someone else's life simply by being available to serve that person. Our hope is that you'll be both inspired and resourced to continue your own coaching ministry in the years to come.

Chapter One

Everyone Needs a Coach
by Ben Wong

I have a dream – "A world where there are no lonely pastors!"

I have always been the active type. I was the youngest of eight, and all my siblings excelled in school. I, on the other hand, did not. In the Chinese culture, this meant that I was "naughty." Instead, I loved to ride bicycles and play sports.

My favorite sport was badminton, since I grew up in Indonesia and badminton was the national sport. "Everybody" there simply knows how to play badminton. No one taught me to play; I just caught on. I was pretty good, but I did not have any guidance to make me better.

When I was fourteen years old, I returned to Hong Kong.[1] At my high school, I tried out for the school badminton team and made it. For the first time in my life, I had a coach, a person who consistently helped me to improve. Three times a week we practiced after school, and the coach spent time training us. I learned that I had to change the way I hit the shuttle (e.g., badminton ball). I was using the power from my arm and elbow, but the power should really come from the wrist. My coach taught me to stretch out my hands straight in the air and hit the shuttle only using my wrist. I also learned to use my feet by taking long strides.

Having a coach in badminton totally changed my game, and I became a much better player. I began to win in competition and became a key player for my school.

What a difference a coach can make!

After graduation, I continued to play badminton. I joined a club where there was a coach and continued to improve. I even paid to have a coach! That was how valuable a coach was to me.

Coaching in Life

Because my mother was a very dedicated Christian, I have been going to church since I was a child. Going to church became a regular routine of my life. When I went back to Hong Kong, I attended the church my sister was going to and went to the youth fellowship. My sister was in the choir, so I joined the choir also. We would practice after Sunday Service, and then we would sing in the choir on Sunday.

Being a Christian was attending all these activities. Some of these activities were fun, but the vast majority were boring. Meeting new girls, in fact, was one of the main attractions for me.

When I was sixteen years old, my parents sent me to Australia.[2] I still attended church because it was what my mother wanted me to do. In other words, being a Christian was not "my" choice; it was my mother's choice. Because of this, I did not consider myself a Christian.

In 1970, during my first year in university, I made a personal decision to receive Christ.

Shortly after I became a Christian, I joined an organization called the Navigators, and they began to help me grow in my Christian life. A fellow Navigator named Doug became my coach and helped me to follow Jesus. He met with me every week for three years, and in the final year I stayed in his home.

What a difference it made to have a coach like Doug! When someone coached me in badminton, I became a much better badminton player. Now I had someone coaching me in the Christian life, and my life was transformed.

Doug helped me to grow in all areas of my life. I was a shy person who did not know how to develop relationships with others. Doug helped me to develop my character. My faith became strong, and foundations were built that have lasted until today.

When I led someone to Christ, Doug would coach me to disciple this new convert. I would then repeat the process on the people that I discipled (i.e. help them to disciple their new converts). This is the way Jesus did it. He chose twelve disciples and trained them to disciple others. This is the normal Christian life.

Coaching Disciples

Many of the ones I discipled in Australia were Malaysian. They had come to Australia to study and afterwards returned to Malaysia.

Recently, I decided to visit some of them, and so I flew to Malaysia. It was such a joy to see them! I had not been with many of them for thirty years. I was thrilled to discover that nearly all of them were living strong, productive Christian lives. Many of them were playing key roles in their churches and ministries.

After thirty years, I can truly say, "coaching people really works." It does make a permanent difference in the lives of people!

However, few Christians have received coaching. Even the pastor of my church in Australia had never been personally coached. He had no one to turn to when facing struggles and needing support.

Coaching as a Pastor

In 1979 I went to seminary and once again was shocked to find out that most of the students had never been coached. Most of them struggled in their Christian lives all by themselves.

The seminary that I attended was not designed for coaching students. Yes, a student could call on a counselor when facing problems, but most didn't have a regular mentor or coach. Then I discovered that most of the seminary professors had never been coached. Nor did they have a desire to coach others, or even learn how to do it.

After seminary, I became a pastor of a church of fifteen people. I felt inadequate and didn't know how to run a church. Most of what I studied for three years was not relevant to what I was facing in ministry, and I often wished that I had someone to turn to for advice and practical help, like a coach who would come alongside me in my journey as a pastor.

The good thing was that I knew how to coach the members of my church and to help them develop Christ-likeness in the lives of others. Looking back, this was the key point of success in my first pastorate. The church grew over 500% in the years I was there.

After six years in this church, I felt called to pioneer a new church with four other people.

We decided to implement one-on-one mentoring for all our

members. Each one would be coached by someone while seeking to coach others.

We felt called from the beginning to focus on reaching the common people of Hong Kong, since the majority of Hong Kong people are lower class with very few churches among them. We wanted to have an integrated church, just like society itself. Since 70% of Hong Kong people are lower class, we wanted that same mix.

Our goal was to proactively win the ordinary people and then to coach them to become extraordinary people.

Today we can say that we have done this well. Most of the leaders in our church are ordinary people that we have trained. Most of the long-term missionaries that we've sent out (numbering close to fifty now) are the same ordinary people that we have coached and seen transformed.

Jo is an example of the transforming power of coaching. [3] She was very rough and young when we got to know her. She lost her mother when she was one year old, and her father was a drug addict. Many people, other than those in her family, raised her. Her anger was so explosive that even boys were afraid of her.

When Jo came to know Jesus, she changed a great deal but still had a lot of rough edges. We took time to invest in her life, and she even stayed in our home for two years. God did wonders in her life.

She became one of the main leaders in our church, and we sent her to a difficult nation as a missionary (one of those places where life is hard, and ministry is even harder). The city she lives in now was chosen as the second worst city to live in. Today, Jo is a very effective mother of four children, and we are all proud of her. We have many like Jo in our church. Coaching is effective and people's lives are changed dramatically as a result.

Pastors Need Coaching

As the church began to grow, we networked with other church pastors. I got to know these pastors and discovered that most of them were struggling. Each one was a one-man-show, and I began to realize that most pastors were lonely people.

While there are some big churches in the world, over 80% of all churches are under 100 members. Sadly, the focus is consistently placed on the biggest and most successful churches, and the smaller ones feel like failures. Most of the pastors of small churches are faithful people, but try as they may, they find it hard to break the 100 barrier. Many of them are hurting because they feel that they have failed.

Four years ago, Catherine, one of the pastors in my church, met another lady pastor, Anna, who had faithfully served God for over twenty years. However, when Catherine met her, Anna was in depression. Every day she would have headaches. She was unhappy, under great pressure, feeling helpless, and with no way out of this trap called pastoring.

She was sent from the mother church ten years earlier to start a new church plant with a group of members. For the first few years, things went well and good growth occurred. Then there was discouragement and conflict. Members left, the attendance dropped, and Anna began to feel a lot of pressure.

The situation worsened when the mother church demanded improvement. They gave the church only twelve months to either improve or close down.

When Catherine met Anna, she was a broken lady (even though she had served God for over twenty years). Catherine cried, "How can the church of Jesus allow this to happen?"

Catherine made a simple decision: "I will walk along side of Anna and do my best to help her." Catherine was not a trained coach but had the heart to reach out and befriend Anna. God used Catherine to restore Anna's confidence and vision.

"Why can't the pastors who are doing better reach out their hands and coach those who are struggling?" I asked myself. "Since we are coaching people in our own church, why not help other pastors who are struggling?"

Coaching cannot be relegated to only experienced pastors (most of them are too busy anyway to help others). We wanted to build a movement where churches reach out and care for other churches, regardless of the size of the church.

There are many seminars and courses on various themes to help pastors and churches, but in my experience, they don't really help pastors.

I've discovered that pastors who can change by listening to a seminar actually do not need the seminars in order to learn and do well. The opposite is also true. Pastors who actually need the seminars will find it very hard to change by listening to a seminar. These pastors need coaches--people who will come along side of them to be a friend. They need someone who can be an inspiration and an example to them.

God began to lay a burden on my heart to coach other pastors, but I didn't know how. I knew how to coach other Christians but not pastors. I had not seen it done before, but I realized that it had to be done.[4] So from 1994, I began my journey into discovering how to coach pastors.

Coaching other pastors has now become a dream and a passion for me. My dream is that every pastor would have a coach, and would then eventually become a coach.

Building an Exemplary Church

We started our church in late 1987 with seven adults and three children. We had no support, no coach, and no physical place to meet. We were willing to learn from anyone willing to teach us. Even though we were tiny, we helped others by sponsoring seminars and trainings.

In 1989, God clearly spoke to me: "First build an exemplary church." I realized that there were many theories, seminars, and teachings, but few working examples. I felt that people needed to see a practical model at work.

We listened to God's voice and worked hard to build a model church, one that wholly trusted in God and was based on people rather than programs. We focused on making disciples and becoming a missionary church.

Jesus said, "The harvest is plentiful but the laborers are few." The focus should be raising up laborers for the harvest. The problem is not the harvest but the lack of laborers. We decided to concentrate on raising up people.

In those years, we learned an important principle: Modeling is very important in coaching. In coaching people, we model with our own lives. When coaching churches, we model with our ministries. Remember: Coaching is best caught rather than taught!

My Church Is Your Church

In 1994, we got the green light from God that it was time to begin helping other churches. We gathered a network of churches that wanted to share information freely and to help others. Seven pastors became the steering committee for this network. We had only one requirement to be on the committee: Serve others with no conditions or strings attached.

Our motto was: "My church is your church and your church is my church--there is only one church and that is the church of Jesus Christ."

We realized that one church could not reach the whole city. When all the churches are strong and thriving, then we would be able to impact the city. The network exists to see this happen.

Pastors often talk about unity on a general level, but we learned that unity in a practical way is prioritizing the interest of other churches as much as we do our own. We realized we needed to help other churches just because they formed part of the church of Jesus Christ. When we consider the other church being just as important as our own, we will reach out and help with no strings attached, just because that church is the church of Jesus Christ.

Our experience, however, is that most pastors come to the network to get something for their own church. They come with a motivation to gain something. When the network has nothing new to give them, they stop coming. We found that if we wanted them to come back, we needed to provide new material or information for them.

Not many churches actually catch the ethos of contributing to someone else's church. Networking for the sake of others is not an idea that is popular with most pastors. This is true not only in Hong Kong but also in the rest of the world.

The exciting thing is that after fifteen years of consistently giving to other churches, the value of "your church is my church" is beginning to take root, and more are willing to contribute now.

If you keep on sowing, you will eventually reap.

My Journey into Coaching Other Pastors

The network committee met monthly to plan conferences, training, and seminars. We developed camps for pastors and offered training on very practical church issues. We invited specific organizations to come and help build-up the network of churches.

I believe those training events helped a lot, but I've come to realize that coaching is even more effective in producing long-term results. Coaching allows us to walk together with individual pastors rather than just pointing the way.

I began to spend more time with pastors who were willing to allow me to coach them. Through spending time with them and their churches, every one of them experienced significant change. This was very encouraging. I had never coached pastors before and had never received specific training on how to coach. Yet, I was willing to reach out and help them in whatever way possible. I felt satisfied that the Lord through me was making a significant difference in their lives and the life of their churches.

God then showed me that I needed to start a coaching-support group for pastors.

Coaching Group

I gathered a few senior pastors into a coaching support group. I told them that we would not meet beyond three years because I wanted to see them multiply rather than having me always leading them. We decided to meet every other week to support and mentor each other.

In the group times we shared our lives and struggles. We shared a lot about our marriages and the need to become better husbands and fathers. We realized that since family is the base of ministry, we had to first succeed at home. We shared about our own personal lives, our walk with God, and how to keep growing.

Often we would try to stimulate each other to rethink our traditional views of the church, so that we could remain on the cutting edge.

I tried to help them build habits of evaluating and examining everything in their lives. I believe that the ability to self-examine and let God speak into our lives is a very important part of growing as a pastor. We need to evaluate what we hear and what we read on the basis of the Word of God.

I spent individual time with some of these pastors and had the opportunity to visit their churches. I discovered that an outsider can often speak more boldly than someone who has been inside the church for many years. My major desire was to help them fulfill their God-given dreams.

Moreover, we had fun together. We established strong ties and friendships, which have lasted until this present time. In the process of being together for three years, we helped each other grow. God transformed us as we spent time together.

One of the main lessons I learned is that "Everyone can benefit from a coaching relationship." We all need a coach. Our lives change when someone comes along side to help us.

We Need More Coaches!

We need a coaching movement. I believe, in fact, that every pastor should have someone who is reaching out to help him or her and walk ing alongside of him or her. We need to see this movement multiply as more pastors catch the vision to coach others.

The following facts come from pastors in the U.S., but in reality, they are being played out in most countries in the world (July 2009): [5]

Pastors' Family
• 80% believe pastoral ministry has negatively affected their families.
• 33% state that being in the ministry is an outright hazard to their family.
Struggle with Inability
• 90% of pastors feel they are inadequately trained to cope with the ministry demands.
• 80% of pastors and 84% of their spouses feel unqualified and discouraged in the role of pastors.
• 90% of pastors said the ministry was completely different than what they thought it would be like before they entered the ministry.
• 50% feel unable to meet the demands of the job.

Struggle with Inability

• 70% of pastors constantly fight depression.

• 70% say they have a lower self-image now than when they first started pastoring.

• 70% of pastors do not have someone they consider a close friend.

• 80% pastors' spouses feel left out and underappreciated by church members.

• 50% of pastors feel so discouraged that they would leave the ministry if they could, but have no other way of making a living.

• 80% of pastors' spouses wish their spouse would choose a different profession.

• Over 1,700 pastors left the ministry every month last year.

These statistics are alarming because they clearly show us that pastors need a coach. Imagine if pastors could turn to someone for help.

- Someone with a listening ear who has walked the same path and understands similar struggles
- Someone who is willing to share his or her experience and be a friend
- Someone who is willing to be a big brother or sister
- Someone who can be an example of how to be a pastor

Most pastors would jump at the opportunity to be coached by someone. The fact is this: Pastors need a coach! "No lonely pastors."

Now, that would be a wonderful dream come true!
I have a dream: "A world where there are no lonely pastors!"

Chapter Two

Dream-based Coaching
by Sammy Ray Scaggs

"Each of us has one...a God-given dream in our hearts of what we can become." -Wayne Cordeiro, Author of "Doing Church as a Team"

It happened! I was in the office of President Sali Berisha, the first democratically elected President of the Republic of Albania. Our meeting was supposed to last ten to fifteen minutes maximum but ended up being forty-five minutes long. We talked about the current events, the challenges facing this new era of Albania, his dreams for this young democracy. I handed him a small Bible in his language, and then I woke up.

Yes, it was a dream that became a real experience within my God-dream to share the Good News with Albanians, a totally unreached people group. That vivid night's dream opened my eyes to the real world of dreams, God-dreams. Little did I know that I would actually fulfill that night's dream two months later in the capital city of Tirana.

In my book The DreamWeaver I talk about "God-dreams" for everyone in general, but in this chapter I want to focus on how God-dreams relate specifically to coaching. I have had good and bad experiences with leaders. My good experiences always seem to center around a discipline that I now call coaching. Another way to describe coaching is intentionally helping leaders stay healthy. Coaching is intentionally being available to see another person change for the good.

Over the years as a leader, I've noticed that my mistakes have helped me to grow, and my victories have also taught me humility by reminding me that God really does want to build His Kingdom through ordinary folks like you and me. He wants to do extraordinary things through ordinary people who make themselves available to His agenda. Being a coach allows me the opportunity to help others get more mileage from both their mistakes and victories.

Coaching is really a discipline that Jesus used long before it became a popular catch phrase in the business world and even in church circles today. It is obvious that Jesus was not only the Master Teacher but also the Master Coach. He asked powerful questions not only to those who were trying to attack Him but also those He loved and served. He listened and reflected on what was happening around Him, and he both challenged and encouraged those He was serving. He is our Master Coach, and we can learn much from His example.

In this book you will see that there are different approaches to coaching, just like there are different styles to teaching and preaching. There is no one way of teaching, and there is no one way of coaching. This is the reason that we believe that everyone in the Kingdom of God can coach someone else. Every pastor can coach another pastor, and every church can coach another church.

However, you will notice that each of the authors in this book is passionate about different key areas. Rather than seeing them in conflict, it is our desire that you see these different areas as complementing each other. For example, you will see in this chapter that I will emphasize asking questions and not giving advice or teaching in the beginning of the coaching relationship for a variety of reasons. As the coaching relationship matures, trust will be strengthened to the point where the coach can offer insights, personal experiences, and principles that will challenge the coachee to consider testing the counsel offered without having to learn the hard way. And like Jesus, a coach may be able to offer a new insight to Kingdom-living that could be a key for his or her life.

When the coachee embraces new truth, whether it is revealed by the Holy Spirit as a personal insight from questions that were asked or by an insight or teaching from a coach, transformation will occur. This is the ultimate goal of any coaching experience. Joel will emphasize tools in the tool box of a coach. Ben will talk about essence or principals from a biblical perspective, and I will focus on coaching from a God-dream perspective. Our goal is the same thing that Jesus had in His coaching strategy--powerful transformation!

In John 14 Jesus talks about His coaching strategy with His disciples. He prepared them for the transition they were going to make from His personal coaching to being coached by the Holy Spirit after His death, resurrection, and ascension to Heaven.

> If you love me, obey my commandments. And I will ask the Father, and he will give you another Advocate, who will never leave you. He is the Holy Spirit, who leads into all truth. The world cannot receive him, because it isn't looking for him and doesn't recognize him. But you know him, because he lives with you now and later will be in you. No, I will not abandon you as orphans—I will come to you. Soon the world will no longer see me, but you will see me. Since I live, you also will live. When I am raised to life again, you will know that I am in my Father, and you are in me, and I am in you. Those who accept my commandments and obey them are the ones who love me. And because they love me, my Father will love them. And I will love them and reveal myself to each of them" John 14:15-21 (NLT).

This is the spirit of coaching. There is power released by the presence of Jesus, which He promised to His disciples and to us. Christ's Words also help us to catch a glimpse of how powerful coaching can be when we simply make the decision at the very beginning of a coaching relationship "to be present" to others we are attempting to lead. Effective coaching means being present physically, emotionally, and in every other way. It involves helping another person to grow or to find his or her way during tough and challenging times.

Great coaching involves some basic tools that anyone can use. You don't need professional coach training to be effective in coaching someone in the Kingdom. You just need the right heart to begin. If we combine the heart of Jesus with the power of the Holy

Spirit (along with some basic coaching skills), virtually anyone or any leader with the right heart and attitude can coach. Yes, it's true. You can coach! Let me begin with a basic step in the right direction – dream-based coaching.

My friend, Wayne Cordeiro says, "Each of us has one. . . . a God-given dream in our hearts of what we can become." If we operate with that belief, then we can successfully coach anyone who wants to learn and grow. And for those who have a God-dream in their heart to expand the Kingdom of God in the world, we can use the discipline of coaching to provide the support, encouragement, and accountability (SEA) they need to see the dream realized.

Did you notice what the first sentence of Chapter One declared? Yes, a dream--a God-dream. One of Ben's God-dreams is that there will be no lonely pastors! In fact, the entire first chapter outlines why hundreds of leaders look to Ben as a coach. In fact, this book you are now holding in your hands was his dream, and I am delighted to be a part of fulfilling this dream to bless and release you in your coaching ministry. Here is what I have to offer, and it is my prayer that it will be helpful to you.

One of the many approaches to healthy coaching is learning how to ask powerful questions. It is a skill that can easily be developed if you work at it. Let's dig a little deeper into this approach of asking powerful questions. In the rest of the chapter we'll look at the definition of biblical coaching, basic disciplines of coaching, implementing the God-dream in real life, as well as servant leadership.

What Is Coaching?

Coaching is primarily for healthy people! Counseling in general is for hurting people. So, being coached and providing coaching does not mean the coachee is weak or unhealthy. In fact, it really means quite the opposite. The Bible is full of examples of dynamic leaders who both provided and received coaching. Think of Moses (coachee) and his father-in-law Jethro (coach). What about Jonathan (coach) and David (coachee), Jesus (coach) and his disciples (coachees), the Apostle Paul (coachee) and Barnabas (coach), and the Apostle Paul (coach) and Timothy (coachee). The list goes on with many more examples. Sometimes we get the impression that coaching is something totally new. However, as mentioned earlier, coaching is not as new as some may think. Coaching is the dedication and discipline of one person coming along side of another person to help him or her become all that he or she can be by assisting him or her to stretch a little more in their leadership development potential. Sometimes a coach can be used to help a coachee articulate the God-dream locked up inside of his or her heart and then define their goals and action steps to actually see the dream realized.

My personal definition of coaching is "mining the gold that is hidden below the surface." This definition was influenced by my friend Pastor Wayne Cordeiro. I believe that every person has a God-dream locked deep down inside of him or her that is extremely valuable, and it is designed to be released in this world for the glory of God. When we apply it to the goal of Kingdom expansion, the rewards are not only eternal, but they are also valued and appreciated in our temporal time on earth.

My organization, Lifeforming Leadership Coaching, defines coaching this way: "The person being coached is the expert who has the answers within himself or herself. Working with a coach allows a person to discover the answers."

Okay, so you want to coach! Where do you begin? Let's look as some basic disciplines of coaching that you can consider using to get started.

Basic Disciplines of Coaching

Know Yourself

Once you catch the vision of coaching, all you need to do is discover your own coaching style and start building upon that. What I mean by "style" is your motivational and ministry gift mix, as well as your DISC profile. A DISC profile is a four-quadrant behavioral model based on the work of William Moulton Marston to examine the behavior of individuals in their environment or within a specific situation. It focuses on the personality styles and preferences of such behavior. DISC is an acronym for:

Dominance -- relating to control, power and assertiveness.
Influence -- relating to social situations and communication.
Steadiness -- relating to patience, persistence, and thoughtfulness.
Conscientiousness -- relating to structure and organization.

Using myself as an example, my spiritual motivational gift is a mixture of leadership and teaching. In addition, my DISC profile is a high D/I depending on whether I am working with other "D's." If I am in a room with other strong "D's" my "D" will drop, my "I" will kick in, and I will defer to another's leadership. Then I let my leadership on the project flow from my relational "I" type. However, I have to use discipline to do this because it doesn't come naturally. I have learned from experience that this works well for me.

This gift mix comes in handy with a public preaching and teaching ministry but has the potential to ruin a healthy coaching relationship if I am not careful. Again, discipline comes into focus. I must make sure that I stay authentic with the way God has designed me and not overpower by my own strength. In the beginning of the coaching relationship, instead of preaching, teaching, and giving advice to the person I am coaching, I intentionally listen, reflect on what is being said, and write down good questions when I am tempted to speak prematurely!

I have discovered that my style gives me the ability to have insights and to be a great source of encouragement. Yet, I still stay true to how God has designed me and can apply powerful coaching techniques for the glory of God. If you do not know what your DISC profile or your ministry gifts are, you can do a simple Internet search for a free online assessment. Once you make these discoveries, you can allow your coaching style to flow from this. You will be glad you did this and so will those you coach.

One of the keys to being a successful coach is to be authentic to who you really are, and then to be an active listener instead of just being an advice giver. Most leaders in the church are aware of their spiritual gifts and personality profile. Since we are aware of who we are, we need to let our coaching style flow out of that authentic style. Another thing that most pastors in the church are good at is preaching and giving advice.

However, this strength can become a weakness when it comes to the discipline of authentic coaching. We are so used to being "on" as leaders, preaching and teaching the Word of God, that we sometimes confuse that role with coaching. We can sometimes end up "telling" those we are "coaching" what to do rather than understanding that the Holy Spirit is at work within them. The answers they most desperately need are just beneath the surface, in His hands. If we would coach them to discover that truth and show them that God has placed His plan and dream in their hearts to do key initiatives for Kingdom expansion, things could change dramatically for the better.

So, how do we coach if we do not tell the coachee what to do in the beginning of the coaching relationship? This is a great question. Let's look at each component to be sure we are thinking from the same perspective.

Active Listening

One of the most important steps is to discipline ourselves to engage in active listening. There are many definitions of "active listening," so allow me to share what I am referring to. When someone is talking to you and sharing his or her heart, many times we listen at the beginning of their message and unintentionally fill in the blanks with what we "think" the person is trying to say. When we practice active listening, we are actually trying to hear the complete message behind the introductory sentences to each subject at hand. Our goal is to engage the individual the same way that Jesus did. He listened to the message behind words and then responded. Sometimes He would say things that would shock those standing by watching the events unfold. Sometimes He would answer questions with questions because He was using this active listening discipline. He is the Master Coach, and observing His interaction with others in the Gospels will give you tremendous insights as to how you can best approach active listening.

Research all over the world is concluding that no matter what culture you and I were raised in, we can improve our listening skills. Recent research indicates that on average we remember 25-50% of what we hear. If I am honest with myself, that is pretty close to what I find myself doing when I am listening casually to someone. Why? Active listening requires focus and energy. It is work, plain and simple. But it is worth it because we can help unlock a dream or create a place of refuge for struggling leaders so they can be released to do what God has called them to do.

My "advice," therefore, is to *listen* to what the person you are coaching is saying and even to what they are not saying! What do I mean by that? Well, when someone is sharing about what I would call a Number 10 issue (a big issue) but uses a Number 3 emotional sentence and attempts to move onto something else, I will take note. And when it is appropriate, I will go back to the statement and start probing with some more open questions. I have discovered that this happens because the person I am talking with is trying to discern if I am really listening or if it is a safe place to share something really important or even risky.

When I go back and pick up on the issue that raised a flag in my mind, the person I am coaching will say something to the effect that they were wondering what my response was going to be. This is why reflecting on what the person says is so important.

When we reflect, we are able to discern what the deeper issues are and allow our curiosity to grow to help the coachee to share more and more information about a particular subject. When we practice this, sooner or later we will assist these leaders to discover and then reveal something they might never uncover by themselves.

I call active-listening a discipline because a thirty-second pause is usually not enough. Sometimes we need to be comfortable with silence – long enough to allow the speaker to go deeper with a particular issue. It takes thought and time for some people to express what and how they feel. Now I don't mean we need to pause for a full minute in absolute silence. I suggest that we remain sensitive to the Spirit's leading to be silent for as long as we need to be in any given situation, allowing the coachee all the time he or she needs.

Active listening requires us to allow enough silence to occur so that someone who is not used to being coached is impressed that you are serious about hearing what they really have to say. You may need to remind yourself to "stop talking" until it becomes more natural.

Let me explain what I mean by that. I am a "recovering advice giver" so I know what I am talking about. Before the coaching relationship would mature, I would lose many great opportunities to learn what God was doing in the life of the coachee because I would be too quick to give advice. I am not saying that giving advice is bad. But if we give it too early we might miss great opportunities to learn crucial information at the very beginning of the coaching relationship.

When we begin to recognize that premature advice-giving is detrimental to becoming an effective coach, we first stop talking on the outside, and then we also have to stop talking on the inside. It is natural when we start new habits that our old habits will resist the change at first. So, once you get the verbal response in check, the very next step is to check the mental dialogue inside of your head. You can do this once you become aware of the process. In fact, becoming aware is usually 75% of the battle. The rest is just practice. Some other things you can do is take notes while the coachee is talking. Begin to write out some questions, and then choose the best question to ask at the precise point of the dialogue.

Again, at the beginning of the coaching relationship, asking good questions is one of the coach's primary roles. What kind of questions do I ask? Let's look at that now.

Ask Powerful Questions

The best place to start is by asking "open questions" and then gradually progress towards asking "powerful questions." When we do this, we begin to "see the lights come on" in those we are helping. We also begin to discover the unique dream that God has placed within the heart of the person we are coaching.

But what is an open question? It is the opposite of a "closed question." We use these all the time, but we may never think about what they are. A closed question is a type of question that provides only a "yes" or "no" answer. An open question allows the hearer the opportunity to say whatever he or she thinks, feels, and believes concerning the question.

If the coach follows up with more and more open questions, the one who is being coached will begin to share things that they usually think about, but have never had the opportunity to express or explore more deeply. Then they start to "see" their thoughts, gain more insights, and even see some solutions to their own challenges. Here are some examples of closed questions and suggestions as to how to make them open questions:

Closed: "Have you asked your spouse about the decision to move to another country?"
Open: "Can you tell me about the process you are using with your spouse to make the decision to move to another country?"
Closed: "Did you react to your team because you were afraid?"
Open: "What personal factors led you to react towards your team in this way?"

Other examples of open questions:
• "What is the most important subject you would like to talk about today?"
• "If there were no barriers, what kind of church would you like to build?"
• "What is the most significant element of the entire experience?"
• "What are some things you could contribute to make a positive change in this relationship challenge?

The next level in asking good coaching questions is asking what we call "powerful questions." Here is my definition of a "powerful question." A "powerful question" is simply an "open question" on steroids! When you ask a powerful question, you will hear the coachee responding with words like, "That is a great question!", "Wow!", or "No one has ever asked me that question before." When you hear statements like that, most likely the person you are coaching will need some time before they respond. This is where we combine active listening with open and powerful questions. A powerful question causes the coachee to stop and respond from their heart. This leads to a deeper discovery. Here are some examples of powerful questions to help you begin creating your own:

- What will you do if your first attempt at this project fails?
- How would a failed outcome affect your attempts to advance in the future?
- What personal-growth change needs to happen in your life for you to move to the next level?
- If you could do this event over again, what changes would you make?
- What steps will you take to overcome this challenge?
- What have you dreamed to do that could change someone else's life?

When those you are coaching start to answer these types of questions, you will think you have hit the "mother lode" of gold because they will start sharing things they have never articulated before. At the end of your session together they will say things like, "Thank you so much! Your time with me has opened new doors of understanding! Your assistance has guided me to a place I have never been before!" Statements like these may surprise you, and you will think to yourself, "I really didn't do anything at all." But in reality you did! You listened, reflected, and you thoughtfully asked open and powerful questions. This is how coaching gets really exciting!

This leads us to our next topic. While listening and asking great questions are important ingredients in the coaching process, it's important to always keep in mind the ultimate goal: to uncover and release the goals, plans, and even the God-dreams.

Positive Affirmation

Everyone needs positive affirmation, especially when it comes to a God-dream to do something different. When we affirm someone's God-dream, it takes discipline, faith, and maturity to listen, ask powerful questions, and then to affirm something not yet visible to the naked eye. Many people equate God-dreams with fantasies. Actually, the two are light-years apart.

Over the years, whenever I have brought up the topic of "God-dreams," I usually get two responses which are on opposite sides of the actual place I would like to go. Some people just dismiss the whole topic of God-dreams because they believe I am referring to a fantasy, something we believe will happen that requires no faith. The other extreme is assuming I am talking about mystical sleep dreams and their interpretations. Even though God used sleep dreams in the Bible to get the attention of key people, I am not referring to them.

Please allow me to share my personal tried and proven guidelines that I use in discerning the difference between a God-dream and a fantasy. As I mentioned, a fantasy requires no faith. It is just a fantasy. But a God-dream requires faith! When someone is born again and filled with the Spirit of God, the God-dream is activated and begins to take shape. Every time you get closer and closer to it, something inside of your soul lights up, and a peace that passes all understanding begins to nudge you closer and closer to your God-given destiny. Here are some guidelines to help you discern between fantasy and faith-inspired God-dreams:

- The God-dream will never contradict scriptural wisdom.
- The God-dream will bring peace to your life, even if it con flicts with worldly wisdom.
- The God-dream can stand the test of discernment and even persecution.
- The God-dream will always be "other focused," not the other way around.
- The God-dream will take time to be realized.
- The God-dream needs the power of God to pull it off.

If you can pull it off in your own strength, then it is most likely not a God-dream.

- The God-dream needs wisdom from God to navigate through the pitfalls and challenges created by it.
- The God-dream will draw fire from the enemy and anyone he chooses to use to hinder and suppress it from being realized.
- The God-dream will have both valleys and mountain top seasons.

This is not an exhaustive list, but these guidelines have helped me as a coach to mine the potential inside of others who had a dream about fulfilling a leadership challenge. This could be starting a new ministry, planting a church, or achieving some other God-sized dream.

Joseph, son of Jacob, is one of the best examples in the Bible of a leader who had a God-dream and then saw it come to pass. Joseph was only seventeen years old when his God-dream began to surface, but it was approximately twenty years later that the dream was realized!

We know that everything begins from a vision in the mind of someone. The clothes you are wearing, the mobile phone you are using, the watch you have on, and even the building you sleep in all began in the mind of someone, somewhere, at some time. Joseph had a God-dream to become a great leader who would influence the lives of many people. Moses had a God-dream to see his people set free to become the nation they were destined to be. Paul had a God-dream to see the Gentiles enter the Kingdom of God. The list goes on and on.

It is the same with your God-dream and the God-dreams of those you coach! These God-dreams have temporal and eternal significance. And when it comes to expanding the Kingdom of God, God's desire is to use ordinary people to reach unsaved people for His glory! We all know that when it comes to expanding the Kingdom the enemy will do everything in his power to stop us. So serving in the role as a coach of other leaders is a noble thing to do, and it could mean the difference between success or failure in a Kingdom initiative.

When our team began to talk about this book and the idea of coaching leaders, I got really excited because when I was serving both at home and abroad, I would have given anything to have had someone coach me with these basic skills.

"Dream-based coaching" is a term that came to mind at the time I was asked to write this chapter. Dream-based coaching is incorporating everything we have talked about up to this point. If you decide to practice the discipline of coaching and operate from a faith perspective that "You Can Coach" and that every person has been endowed with a "God-dream" inside of them just waiting to be realized, then all things are possible!

Sadly, I have seen well-meaning leaders try to impose a nonbiblical vision on someone else. Or perhaps they saw a successful ministry in action and then tried to get others to copy that ministry, even though their culture and context was not compatible. When ministry initiatives fail, leaders sometimes pull back, never again to attempt great things for God. What I love about coaching with biblical principles is that they always transcend culture, and the methodology used can be different when applying the same principle.

So, if a leader fails at an initiative, we can coach him or her to learn from the failed outcome. We can coach the leader to do as John Maxwell challenges: to learn to "fail forward"! Life and leadership are full of challenges and failed outcomes, but we can learn from them. And we can help those we coach to move on from each experience, no matter what the outcome of those experiences has been. We can help the coachee grow and mature from those challenges and become all that God wants them to become!

What are some key questions that can assist us in coaching leaders and help them to begin the whole dream unpacking experience? My friend, coach, and mentor in this particular area is Doug Fike. Doug has authored our "Life Focus" Training Track, as well as other training materials that have helped hundreds of leaders get in touch with their God-dreams and destinies. Here are some of his key questions:

- What positive or negative life circumstances have shaped you in fundamental ways?
- What kinds of needs (situations, circumstances, or people needs) really tug at your heart?
- What have others seen and affirmed in you?
- What are you naturally gifted at?
- What do you think you've been called to do?
- What are the significant places where God has spoken to you about your life purpose?
- Which of the previous areas have you seen converge together at different points in your life?
- What happened when this occurred in your life?

Questions like these will help those you coach begin to discover some of the clues that will point them in the right direction of their God-dream, their destiny, and even their clear purpose in life! This is what makes coaching such an exciting and rewarding role.

However, like any role, you must have the right heart for it to be life-giving. Having the heart of the Master Coach, Jesus, is critical. Anything we do for Him – our model – involves the heart of a servant. That is the subject we want to focus on now by providing examples of Dream-based coaching.

Examples of Dream-based Coaching

Several years ago I had the opportunity to coach a man who had left the leadership team of another church and had clearly discerned that God was calling him to plant a new church from scratch. Although he had served on several teams in a secondary role, he had never planted a church as the primary leader.

This time he was the primary leader with a vision to plant and lead this church. It was a bit sobering because he was now in a position to act upon his God-dream that had been growing in his heart for many years. It's like a father or mother who dreamed of the day they would have a child of their own. When the child finally arrives, reality suddenly settles in. It is no longer theory or imagination; it is the real thing! A leader can become paralyzed not only from being told what to do but also by not knowing how to activate the dream God has given him or her for this new church that only exists inside his or her heart. A skilled coach is needed in assisting leaders to do the things that God has laid on their hearts to do. Remember: You Can Coach!

That is what I did with Kurt. I started by asking him to tell me specifics about what the church would look like after its birth. I asked him, "Kurt, if there were absolutely no barriers to building this church what would it look like five, ten, fifteen years from now? Who are the people attending this church? What are their ages? Are children and teenagers included? What would the worship services look like? What specific mission would this church family have that would make it unique?" Questions like this guided our conversations in person and over the phone for several months. It was exciting to watch his eyes light up as he talked about this church that was planted within his heart. As he responded to these questions, I got excited about this church. I took notes and continued to ask even more questions as he shared in greater detail about this church and the things that God could do.

Today I can honestly say that he is right on track with his God-dream for his church. It is alive, growing, and thriving, and it looks just like the church he described to me when we talked on that summer day under the shade of a tree, with the doors of the car open. Kurt has a healthy team of elders and ministry leaders, and his church has taken shape according to his dream of a released congregation that is reaching children and adults for Jesus, both in his own country and around the world!

This passion for coaching comes from being personally transformed by key coaches in my life. One of them is Ben Wong, who was there for me when I was going through one of the most difficult times in my life and felt very alone and isolated. I was thinking about quitting the ministry, but Ben kept coming back into my life – asking me powerful questions and challenging me to "keep looking up." On one occasion, Ben called me for one of our "coaching sessions," and we talked for over an hour.

Finally, I asked him where he was calling from since we had talked for so long. I assumed he was somewhere within my country. (This was before we had Skype and free Internet phone calls.) His answer was, "I live in Hong Kong." I was shocked when I discovered that he was coaching me from the other side of the world. I told him that he was crazy to spend so much time and money on phone calls from so far away. I will never forget his response. He said very politely, "You are more important than my phone bill." That conversation changed my life. I started "looking up" again. Today I am in a very healthy place because of Ben's coaching.

It is my prayer that many will say the same thing about you one day because of your coaching. I pray over you right now that God will use you to transform others lives and that you will see them as more important than your phone bill or anything else that might stand in your way

Where Do You Go from Here?

This chapter was designed to impress upon your mind that "You Can Coach!" We wanted to stimulate your thinking to consider using "Dream-based coaching" as one of the many tools in your coaching tool box. We also looked at some basic coaching methods that you can use to begin coaching today. This is just one small step. Joel and Ben will assist you with other tools and approaches as you turn the page and continue your discovery. If you want to discover more about God-dreams, check out my website: www.Ps139DreamWeaver.com.

Remember: You can coach!

The Coaching Toolbox
by Joel Comiskey

n 2001, I started coaching pastors fulltime.[6] There was one problem. I didn't know how to coach. I thought I knew, but in reality, I equated coaching with giving advice. As a result, my coachees were not responding well. I have always asked for evaluations, and they were becoming more and more negative. I even had some leaders who were so frustrated with me that they released me from further coaching obligations. It was one of the most difficult times of my life.

The good news was that I could only move upwards. I began to devour every piece of literature on coaching. An entirely new way of coaching opened up to me. The gracious leaders that stuck through my trials welcomed my changed perspective, and they found that I had something to give.

I learned, for example, the importance of listening. Previously, I thought I had to impress the coachee with my wisdom and answers. But I realized that my job was to primarily draw the answers from the coachees. I learned about the importance of asking powerful questions and the importance of encouraging and empowering leaders.

I developed a framework for my coaching based on listening, questioning, encouraging, and helping the coachee find answers for him or herself. I even asked an experienced coach to counsel me about how to coach. I met with him often, and he instructed me on basic coaching principles. He kept pressing me, for example, to remember that coaches, like myself, should not be quick to teach, consult, or give advice. Rather, they should place the coachee in the driver's seat and simply guide the discussion through questions.

My coach, as well as other experts in coaching, was quite dogmatic about what a coach should or should not do. I repeatedly learned that my main job was to draw answers from the coachee. The coachee had to make the decision for him or herself. The role of the coach was to ask questions to guide the coachee to make his or her own decisions.

I began to practice this 100%. I would not give advice. If the pastor asked me a question, I would turn it around and ask a question back, "What do you think you would do?"

Learning from Feedback

As I implemented these coaching patterns, I discovered that some of my coachees were frustrated because I was not providing teaching and direct answers. Since I asked the pastors for regular oral and written feedback, I learned that some wanted *more than* listening and powerful questions. Yes, they liked the listening part, but they also wanted my expert advice and knowledge. I could ask and ask, but the bottom line was that often they simply didn't know the answer. They needed skilled input as well.

I began to realize that if I was truly going to serve these pastors, I needed to give them what they needed, which often included consulting, teaching, and training. Yes, listening, encouraging, and asking questions continued to be the basis for my coaching, but I needed to expand the scope of my coaching to meet their needs.

I had to be willing to listen, teach, consult, encourage, challenge, and really do whatever it took to minister to my coachees.

When I started opening up the horizons of my coaching, the coachees gave me high marks in my evaluations. They began to like my coaching and even recommend me as a coach.

Using Everything in the Toolbox

I've learned that I have to do what it takes to make the coachee successful. I've termed this concept, "throwing out the rulebook" or put more positively, "using everything in the toolbox." This is probably the most important discovery I've made about coaching.

I've discovered that sometimes I have to confront and challenge.

Other times, I listen to their concerns about cell church, ministry in general, or personal struggles. I have found that there are times when I need to tell them to go back and re-read a book that has all the answers to their concerns. I've learned to create new approaches as circumstances arise.

I have found that I have to bring my entire self to the table when coaching. I'm not just focusing on one aspect of my life but the entire spectrum (e.g., personality, upbringing, cell experience, and knowledge). Whatever I can draw from, I use. I'm not just pulling out my PowerPoints, my cell notes, or coaching rules; I'm giving my entire self.

My goal is to serve the pastor, and so I ruthlessly place his or her agenda as the top priority. I'm sure this is also true in coaching a sport like tennis. ESPN wrote about coaching tennis stars, like Federer, saying,

> In today's game, most players -- top stars as well as journeymen -- put great stock in having a full-time dedicated coach as an appendage. The role of a coach can vary from tactician and strategy expert to psychologist, travel agent, babysitter, substitute parent, and best friend, and often is comprised of all those facets. [7]

The phrase "all of those facets" is critical. There's no one way to do coaching. The best coaching is comprised of "all of those facets." For example, I spend a lot of time praying, listening, and waiting on God before I coach. I bring my spiritual life to the table. I also bring my own character and my relational skills. How I relate to people will come out in my coaching. I also bring my friendship. Sometimes, the most important thing I can do is engage in light-hearted conversation, laughter, or just have fun together.

While coaching, I relate what has worked for me and what has not worked for me, but I also share knowledge of what others have done, books written on the topic, and online information that often goes beyond what I've tested or personally experienced. Often an illustration will jump out at me, and I share it with the one I'm coaching.

Coaching is not all about the coach. It's really about the pastor/coachee. Coaching is getting out of the way and allowing the coachee to share, communicate, and make decisions. The coach's job is to guide that experience.

Variety of Leaders and Situations

I coached one church planter who saw me as a supervisor. This particular pastor was a sharp, independent thinker. He wanted to make his own decisions. He appreciated the in-depth study I did of his life and church plant. He also liked my questions, listening, and encouragement. Since he was not connected with an outside denomination, he saw me as an accountability authority in his life. I moved him onward through asking questions.

I coached another pastor who wanted an in-your-face approach to coaching. This pastor wanted me to confront him and even tell him what to do. Another pastor wanted a combination approach. One was so relaxed that any style would have worked. He just wanted me to hang out enough to make the coaching experience worthwhile.

One church staff wanted me to teach them using PowerPoints over the phone for a time period. Between the teaching times, I asked questions, listened, and resourced them.

I coached another pastoral team that preferred asking me a list of questions each time we came together for coaching. I could have turned their questions around asking, "What do you think?" but the fact is, they were coming to me with questions, and they wanted answers. Servanthood required answering their questions and training them through the question/answer methodology. Of course, I did ask questions, practiced active listening, and sought to encourage this pastoral team.

Pastors are on such distinct places in their journey that one coaching technique simply doesn't fit all. The key is to evaluate each situation and not be content until the pastor is satisfied with your coaching style.

As I coach each pastor, I need to realize that I'm moving in and out of so many distinct cultures and experiences. I'm often jumping back and forth between the personalities of each pastor, even on the same day.

Naomi, an experienced coach in Hong Kong, shared at the CCMN Hong Kong summit in 2008 about her coaching experience. She said that she had to adapt to each situation. Some months she is more of a counselor. Other months she exercises mentorship, or teaching, or just listening. She has come to realize that coaching is all these things wrapped into one. It's not just about one discipline, but it's a variety of actions and activities. "Naomi really understands coaching," I said to myself as I heard her speak.

The coach of pastors wears all and every hat necessary to get the job done. God gives wisdom to help the coach know what to focus on at any given time.

Get to Know the Leader

I seek to know the person I'm coaching, meditating on the person's life and ministry , which I gather into a document I call a *case study*. Some of my case studies become very extensive. I write down every possible fact I discover about the coachee, such as background, personality, family, church information, church doctrine, philosophy, and cell church ministry--or lack of it. I try to observe the pastor, listen to what he or she says, and then document what I hear.

As I prepare for each coaching meeting, whether a phone conversation or face-to-face meeting, I review the case study first. I try to remember what we talked about the last time. I then jot down questions I want to ask the leader. I'll target points of need, past prayer requests, and future goals. However, I'm prepared to respond in an appropriate way if I sense an immediate need or problem.

After the meeting, I make sure to document things I've learned. I then use that information as a resource for prayer and preparation for the next meeting.[8] My normal preparation routine is:
- Look at notes from the last meeting.
- Think and pray through the areas I want to probe.
- Prepare the actual questions.

Bedrock Foundation of Coaching

It seems to me that the bedrock foundation for coaching is servanthood. The coach is the servant. The coach is trying to place the coachee in the driver's seat. The coach doesn't lord over the one being coached but attempts to wash his or her feet. The coach draws out the wisdom that already resides deep within the coachee. The one being coached may already know what's going on but often can't sort it out. The coach pinpoints the problems and brings them to the surface.

Servanthood requires doing whatever it takes to make the coachee successful. The best way to do this is through listening, asking questions, encouragement, and challenging the one being coached to fulfill his or her vision. Yet, the coach should not hesitate to use other instruments in the toolbox, always focusing on the question, "How can I best serve the one being coached?"

Following the Spirit of God

Ultimately, the Spirit of God must lead coaches. Before I coach, I seek to listen to the Spirit of God and find His direction. I realize I need to completely trust God and His grace when I'm coaching.

While I'm listening to the coachee, I'm also listening to the Spirit of God. Listening to both the coachee and the Spirit allows me to flow into a wide range of disciplines and to meet specific needs.

I constantly attempt to improve my coaching through reading and observation, but ultimately the Spirit of God must bring to my attention the principles that are the most important.

I've found that coaching is tougher than seminar speaking because so many more disciplines have to be utilized in the coaching session. A seminar speaker dispenses knowledge, prepares a great PowerPoint, and attempts to balance the event. Coaching is more subtle. Coaching requires every part of the coach's life and ministry to come through. Coaching is much more intuitive. The coach must trust the Holy Spirit's prompting and truly believe that God is leading.

I do not approach my coaching contact times with my own agenda. Rather, I remain completely dependent upon God to guide every thought during my coaching.

I come to each coaching situation on my knees and praying that God would help me to minister to the coaches. He's the Master; I am His instrument!

Coaching Is an Art

Coaching is not a hard-science. It's an art. As I prepare for each coaching appointment, I sense the importance of getting ready to have just the right word for that particular person.

I prepare myself. I study the coachee. I'm ready to the best of my ability. My blood starts flowing quickly. I'm nervous. Everything is in high gear as I prepare for the coaching appointment.

Ultimately I coach to the best of my ability. That's all anyone can do. When the coaching moment arrives, I know I've done the best I can do to prepare myself. And that's all that God requires of me.

Coaching is a mix that is not easily understood. The coach must have the listening mix, the empathy mix, and the teaching mix. Coaching is trying to find the right mix for the coachee. It's not always clear and concise. There's not an easy 1,2,3 sense to it. Each person is different. I don't believe, in fact, that a coach ever fully arrives. Rather, it's a continual learning process.

I know when I've coached well because I feel it. Other coaches can testify of that same feeling. I don't know if great coaching is definable. It just happens. It's an ongoing relationship. Every time I get on the phone with a pastor, I'm becoming vulnerable. I'm trying to make something work—we're in the process. Because I'm growing as a person, I'm always changing. Coaching is ultimately Joel Comiskey giving all he has.

The coach can easily think that he or she has wired the art of coaching. Easy. Presto. Yet, it's just at the point of supposedly "figuring it out" that the coach might start sinking. It's probably best to feel inadequate so that our inadequacy compels us to depend on the Lord. Only Jesus can make it work. Only Jesus can change people and fulfill goals and desires that have eternal benefits.

Coaching remains in the realm of mystery. There's no secret formula to working with people. Yes, it's harder this way, but I suppose that's the way it should be. I've had magical moments, and

I've had very hard moments. I've been high in the clouds and down in the depth. It's best to keep coaching in the realm of mystery, so we always learn to depend on Jesus Christ for success.

Evaluations will show how the coach is doing. In fact, I often don't know how I'm doing as a coach until I receive my regular evaluations from the coachees (more on this later).

Freely Giving to Others

Coaching is marked by a friendly, giving spirit. The coach should be ready to pass on knowledge in a friendly, loving way. The coach needs to be willing to give everything and be completely open and honest.

A good friend of mine, René Naranjo, a very successful architect in Ecuador, once told me that he always tried to exceed the expectations of those who bought homes. He wanted those buying homes from him to tell their friends, thus creating a snowball effect. This generous attitude has worked wonderfully for René because in a country of poverty and problems, René has always had plenty of work—even beyond what he could accept.

Scripture says in Proverbs 11:25, "A generous man will prosper; he who refreshes others will himself be refreshed." I believe in providing information freely. I must give, give, and give some more while expecting nothing in return. I must not hide anything. Everything is on the table. Generosity reigns. Stinginess is out of the question. The more I can give, the better. My coachees receive everything I have.

Paul said in Acts 20:17-21:

> From Miletus, Paul sent to Ephesus for the elders of the church. When they arrived, he said to them: "You know how I lived the whole time I was with you, from the first day I came into the province of Asia. I served the Lord with great humility and with tears, although I was severely tested by the plots of the Jews. You know that I have not hesitated to preach anything that would be helpful to you but have taught you publicly and from house to house. I

have declared to both Jews and Greeks that they must turn
to God in repentance and have faith in our Lord Jesus.

One time in Slovakia, missionary Kevin Wood, asked me about
my methodology of coaching. I shared with him the concept of
using everything in the toolkit and freely sharing everything with
the coachee. Kevin, who received his doctoral degree in counseling,
agreed 100% with my method of coaching. He said, "Counseling as
a profession is more and more steering away from the "therapeutic
listening" model to offering advice and holding the counselee to
that advice." While coaching is different from counseling, we both
agreed that a coach shouldn't hesitate to do whatever it takes to
minister to the coachee.

If we love people we will give them everything we know. The
key is how we share the knowledge. If we do all the talking, we'll
never really know if the one being coached has internalized the
information. Often the best teaching method is asking questions
because when the coachee answers for him or herself, their ideas
may stick.

Yet, it's easy to fall into the trap of not freely teaching and giving
needed information when the coach is only listening. The fact is
that the one being coached needs information to achieve personal
improvement.

A Few Steps Ahead

I learned how to coach through coaching. I grew as I coached. I
failed and learned from my mistakes. I'm still learning. Coaching is
still pioneer effort, and that's why I'm constantly asking the coachee
to tell me how I'm doing. I need to know. I need to understand.

We grow in our coaching ability as we get out there and coach.
Being involved in the battle is the best way to learn and grow.

The coach has experienced ministry sufficiently to pass on his
knowledge to others. I'm inferring that the coach is one step ahead
of the individual he is coaching. Notice that I didn't say a lot further
ahead. I said one step ahead.

You don't need to be a lot further ahead. You do need to be a little bit ahead. A great coach should have played the game at one time. It doesn't mean that he or she was super successful—just experienced. Some are under the impression that the coach must be as good or better than those he's coaching. Untrue. The coach of cell pastors needs to establish a solid track record of helping pastors make it. He needs to be able to point to those who are stronger as a result of his or her coaching.

The great sports coaches are strategists who love the game and have played the game. However, what's great about them is their strategic thinking, knowledge, personality, and leadership. They know how to move a team on to the next level.

As a coach, your job is to take the person to the next level. To do so, you must use all the tools in your toolkit.

Evaluating What Works

How does the coach know if he or she has done a good job? The only way I know is by receiving regular evaluations.

Before I start coaching someone, I ask them to commit to a quarterly evaluation. I rotate those evaluations between oral and anonymous. At the end of the first three-month quarter, for example, I will personally ask each coachee if they have any suggestions or critiques for me (oral evaluation). I write down whatever they say. At the end of the next three month quarter, I send out an evaluation sheet (anonymous evaluation). In the appendix, I give more detail about each of these evaluations, and I even include a sample copy of the anonymous evaluation.

Asking for regular evaluations helps ensure that the coachee is not bottling up hidden criticisms or concerns. It will help the coachee to know that he or she will have an opportunity to express concerns as well as positive feedback. Most of all, a regular evaluation will help the coach to fine-tune his or her coaching.

Chapter Four

Principles We Have Learned in Coaching by Ben Wong

One of the great dangers in coaching is thinking that you need to be an expert before starting on the coaching journey. I did not wait until I was a "perfect" father before I started the fathering journey. I became a father, and then had to learn how to "father" in the process.

We also just stepped out and started coaching, and learned while practicing the principles, even though we didn't have the formal training behind us.

I've never followed a coaching book, telling me what to do. I learned while doing, and I'm still learning in the process of coaching. I don't believe, in fact, that a person ever arrives at a place of perfect coaching.

Most of those coaching today don't have a degree in coaching, but are putting into practice what they've learned.

Over the years, we have learned some basic principles that can help you do a better job of coaching. These principles will give you a head start, but you will still need to learn most lessons in the battle. Just make sure you step out in faith and get started. Even these principles will make a lot more sense while you're practicing them.

Coaching is Serving – Not Controlling

Coaching is not about dominating others (expanding one's influence over others). It's not about building a bigger empire. Rather, it's about serving others wholeheartedly.

Coaching is not expanding one's influence over others. It's not building a bigger empire. Coaching, rather, is serving others wholeheartedly.

I've noticed a trend among some mega-churches to try to corral smaller churches under their umbrella (or "covering" is a more popular word), while calling them "affiliated churches" or some other dignified term. Some mega-churches even require smaller churches to change their name, while others allow the name to stay intact, as long as they are fulfilling all the other rules.

Of course, some of them even require you to pay a percentage of your annual income to them for "administration costs." In return, the mega-church provides coaching and resourcing, but most likely the affiliate church will have to go to the mega-church to learn how things are done "the correct way," or "our way." A few even go to the extreme of imparting their special "anointing" before the church can do any type of ministry.

It is easy to go this way because nearly everyone is doing it. I even found myself several years ago wanting to go that route. I shared with my leadership team that we needed to clarify the type of relationship we had with all the churches that networked with us. I wanted to categorize them according to their degree of commitment to us. We were going to have daughter churches, affiliated churches, network churches, and other categories.

We made the decision to do this and brought it to the entire congregation. Everyone seemed excited. However, God placed an uneasiness in my heart.

One day, my closest associate asked me, "Ben, how come nothing has happened about our new vision." I told him that somehow I did not have peace about going ahead with it, even though it was my idea. I told him that I decided to listen to my heart and hold off any action.

Then I asked him, "How about you? How do you feel about this?" He said that he was uneasy about it from the beginning, but did not tell me because I was so enthusiastic about the whole thing. Then I asked around and quite a few of the key leaders were hesitant about the vision.

In the end, we decided to scrap the new vision. To this present time, we don't clarify who is who in the network.

Coaching stems from the understanding that the New Testament is under the headship of Jesus. Coaching is recognizing that we are all a part of the whole body of Christ. Coaching is catching the Spirit of Jesus who came to serve and not to be served. Coaching is not caring about "my church" but caring about "our church." Even though this is radical thinking for our day, it is the right biblical thinking that we all should have.

In the same way, the coach should never try to control the "coachee." [9] He should not attempt to dictate what the coachee must do: "You must do what I say." On the contrary, the coach's task is to serve the coachee. The coach is to help the coachee understand the biblical essences of the church and then to allow the Spirit to guide.

The coach should not try to benefit himself or herself but to benefit the coachee. This is the reason why in our coaching network we volunteer our coaching service. With us, a pastor doesn't have to pay to be coached. In reality, most of these pastors who need coaching are pastoring very small churches, and it would be very difficult for them to pay a coaching fee.

Moreover, the East Asian culture already feels obligated to repay the coach for the service, so we emphasise the point that there is no cost and no obligation in receiving coaching--except to "pay it forward" to someone else in the future. As Jesus said, "Freely you have received, freely give" (Matthew 10:8).

Coaching Is about the Whole Person

Since the church is all about people, we need to focus our leadership efforts on building them up. If we fail to disciple the members of the church to follow Jesus with their lives, then we fail as the church. In order to help make disciples, we must become interested in the whole life of the person--not just how he or she performs in the activities of the church.

Since the church is all about people, we need to focus on building them up. If we fail to disciple the members of the church to be actual followers of Jesus, then we fail as the church. In order to help make disciples, we must become interested in the whole life of the person, not just how he performs in the activities of the church.

In the same way, when we are coaching a pastor, we need to be concerned with the whole person, and not only how he or she does ministry. In reality, it's impossible to divorce a person from ministry, even though we have tried hard to do so in the church. Coaching pastors must take care of the whole being!

From experience, nearly every pastor I have coached (or have met through the coaching networks) has never had someone care for his or her personal development. When a coach shows interest in this area of the coachee's life, they express surprise and appreciation that someone really cares for them.

Most pastors are struggling with relationships both at home and in the church. Relationship with the leadership (either staff or lay leaders) is a typical problem. Helping a pastor break through to victory is very important.

Another area of need among pastors is to improve their relationship with their spouse and children. This is a constant struggle for pastors, but they usually don't have anyone to turn to for help.

East Asian cultures are shame cultures. We are brought up with our parents drumming into us the importance of not bringing shame to the family. That is why we must do our best to perform well in everything that we do--especially in school. If we do not do well, we bring shame to our family.

Failure is very hard for us to deal with. Failure is shame. It is very hard for us to admit that we are wrong or that we need help. The Chinese have a saying: "The shame of family must not be known outside of the family!" People outside the family should never know of problems happening on the inside. That is why it is very hard for us to seek help when there is hardship in our marriage or family.

In our coaching networks, the coaches openly share about the struggles in their own lives (including family life). Open sharing always has a great impact on the pastors attending. At least 50% of pastors find that one of the greatest blessings of being a part of the coaching network is transparent sharing about family relationships.

Jack [not his real name] was a typical top-down leader, having been taught this model his entire ministry life. As a pastor, he ran the church by himself and made all the decisions personally. People who did not agree with him either kept quiet or left the church.

He governed his household in the same way. There was little to no communication at home. The relationship between him and his wife was at the verge of disintegrating because his wife had become depressed. She felt like her husband never tried to understand her or the children. The church always came first, and the family had no say in it.

The coaching network changed that situation. Jack went home with a new understanding of the church as a family. He realized he had been neglecting his own family. He began to honor his wife and children. His marriage took a turn for the better, and both began coming to the coaching network seminars with a big smile on their faces.

Asian pastors need biblical habits to offset the bad habits inherited from the culture. One biblical habit is to think positively rather than negatively. Most of our culture is exceedingly negative. When we think of others, we dwell on the negative. Even when we pray for people, we are thinking of all the negative things in their lives. Negativity is probably the biggest destroyer of relationships for us.

However, the Bible gives us a new culture--a new way of life. Paul says, "Summing it all up, friends, I'd say you'll do best by filling your minds and meditating on things true, noble, reputable, authentic, compelling, gracious—the best, not the worst; the beautiful, not the ugly; things to praise, not things to curse." [10]

Filling our minds with new things (positive and good things) and meditating on them is a new habit we all need to establish.

Only a small percentage of Christian leaders finish the race victoriously today. Robert Clinton mentioned from his study of leaders that less than one in three leaders finish well, and the number is even less today. In his study of hundreds of Christian leaders who finished well, he identified six characteristics that helped them finish well. [11] All these characteristics have to do with the life of the leader.

We all need to be accountable to one another, so that we can finish well. Integrity of life is critical for the pastor. One of the biggest traps for a pastor is deception! The pastor can become a stage personality, always looking good on the stage but a totally different person off the stage. It is so easy to be a fake. The problem is that some pastors convince themselves that because they talk about ideals, they are actually living those truths. In reality, they are only deceiving themselves. Scripture tells us, *"The heart is deceitful above all things and beyond cure."* [12]

Coaching has to deal with the life of the person. Of course, in dealing with someone else's life, it always reflects our own life, and the coach also has to change.

We need to build trusting relationship between the coach and the coachee. The coaching network needs to have the atmosphere of "we are family." We need to trust each other and feel the security that each of us brings. We need to develop an atmosphere of trust, so that we can freely share everything and not be afraid of judgment.

Church is all about life, rather than methods, so we need to be open to deal with life. There is no shame to admit we need to grow in a certain area of life. There is no shame to admit that we have failed. Failure is the mother of success.[13] If we have failed, we can fail with dignity if we take time to discover the lesson to be learned in the failed outcome.

Coaching Is a Priority

Spending time with the coachee is essential. We cannot build relationships without taking time to be with one another. Taking time means making a coaching commitment.

Tommy had never been trained as a coach, but when he was asked if he would like to coach other pastors, he said "yes" immediately. He is not a famous pastor, and not many people know him. He does not have a big church, but he was willing to be a coach.

Today, Tommy is one of the best coaches I know in Japan, and he is also an inspiration to other pastors. He has a real heart to coach. He treats the coachees as his friends. He and his wife together spend time with the coachees and their wives. They are there when the coachee has a crisis. The coachees say that they've never had someone who cared for them as much as Tommy. One coachee said, "If it were not for Tommy, I would have given up on being a pastor already. He has been such a great friend to me."

In the beginning, many coaches saw caring for another pastor as a good idea, and they committed to become coaches. However, it was not a high priority for them. It was more like a job.

During the evaluation time, these same coaches would often say they had been very busy and did not have sufficient time to meet with the coachee. Some called the coachee once or twice within the month or did not bother calling at all.

On the other hand, for the few years we've been in the coaching network, we are seeing many coaches who truly value coaching like Tommy. They understand that coaching is not an optional extra for them. They realize that coaching is a part of the Church of Jesus Christ, and they are taking more time to go and meet with the coachees and minister to them.

Since the coaches in the coaching network have nothing to gain monetarily through their coaching, their commitment and time is a heart motivation.

Coaching Is Relationship

The coach must become a friend to the coachee. Before talking about ministry, the coach needs to build a relationship with the coachee.

Mark was not even a relational person, but he was captured by the heart to coach other struggling pastors. Now coaching is a passion for him. He spends a lot of time away from his church while coaching pastors, but his church is better off now than before because many of his members have risen up and taken responsibility.

The amazing thing is how Mark has changed to become a relational person. He has changed through his deep desire to help other struggling pastors. The realization that coaching takes place through a relationship and that the first essence of the church is relationship has given him a great deal of motivation to change. He is still young but is actively coaching in his region.

God has called us to enjoy our relationship with Him and others. Yet, many pastors in my part of the world do not know how to enjoy life with God and others. Therefore, ministry to them is not enjoyable either. We know that we have problems if:

- We are not enjoying our life in our marriage.

- We are not enjoying our life in our family.
- We are not enjoying life as a person.
- We are not enjoying our life with our people.

If these things are true, then ministry is not enjoyable or fun. One of the key roles of the coach is to help the coachee relax and have fun!

Many Japanese pastors do not even take a day off. They don't even take the holidays off! They feel guilty when they are having fun. Yet, in reality, enjoying life and relationships are so important for them.

Coaching Is Encouraging

John Maxwell says:

> Everyone needs encouragement. And everyone – young and old, the successful or less-than-successful, unknown or famous – who receives encouragement is changed by it. Encouragement's impact can be profound. A word of encouragement from a teacher to a child can change his life. A word of encouragement from a spouse can save a marriage. A word of encouragement from a leader can inspire a person to reach her potential." [14]

Everyone need encouragement. However, it is not an Asian thing to affirm others. We are basically negative and focus on affirming the weaknesses of others but not the good. We are experts in pointing out people's shortcomings. Most pastors have so much demand put on them. It seems impossible for the pastor to satisfy his congregation, so he always feels like something is wrong with him.

For someone to believe in a pastor, encourage him, and actually bring out the best in him is truly a miracle. If the coach is an encourager, then he will be such an important person in the life of his coachee. Most people do not need more knowledge. Rather, they simply lack confidence. They lack confidence that they are valuable and useful in the hands of the Lord. They need to be built up so that their confidence level will increase.

One Chinese term for encourage is to "pump air," to inflate. When we encourage, we are pumping air into the person so that he or she can stand up and be strong. The opposite is to deflate, or to make the person soft and weak so that there is no strength to even stand up.

Even expressing love to the coachee is such an encouragement to him or her. East Asians are not good at expressing love. Within our culture we do not touch each other when expressing greetings. Rather, we just bow. Many people have never experienced unconditional love; they grow up with love that is very conditional and performance-based.

Love—not theory—builds a person up. By loving the coachee, he or she can love his or her members in the same way.

In one of the coaching network seminars, we shared the first essence about how relationship is the key for the church. We shared how important it is to express love. We demonstrated how to hug someone and asked them to practice on one another (those of the same sex). In the following three months, the coach was expected to follow up on how the coachees had applied the essences of what they had learned.

One of the coachees went back and shared the message with her church. She had experienced hurt with another couple on the leadership team. During the message, she hugged the wife of the couple and shook the hands with the man. The Lord began to work, and they burst out crying. The rest of the congregation began to hug one another, and God did a major thing in that church that day. What happened? Just a simple act of obedience to express love to one another. That is the power of encouragement.

Coaching Is Drawing on Many Resources

It is important to realise that we belong to the same church, and that we are not alone. Even as a coach, we have the resources of the whole network to draw on. All the other coaches are resources for us. All the churches of the other coaches are resources for us.

Since we are part of a network, we must learn to function as such. One coach is limited. The experiences of one coach is minimal.

That is why the coaching network is such a wonderful idea.

In the Hong Kong coaching network, coaches are joined together in small groups. Those coaches in the same small group began to do coaching together and discovered that they all have different strengths. Working together has enriched the coaching experience and has given coachees much more of a variety of help as their pooled resources are greater.

When I am mentoring an individual in my church, I often expose that person to others who are stronger in different areas. I cannot be an example in every area of life to the person I am coaching. I need the body of Christ to do this. For instance, in my church, I have a good friend, Malcolm, who is strong in evangelizing people. He is good at naturally sharing the gospel in conversation with others, and so I like to expose people to Malcolm. I've found that a couple of hours with Malcolm can open up someone's eyes in a way that I could never do. A coach must not be threatened by other pastors who are better than he or she is in some areas of ministry and life.

Using what other people are doing can also be achieved through books, materials, Internet articles, sermons, and many other resources. The key principle is not to limit the coaching to your own talents, experience, knowledge, and gifting.

Coaching Is Helping the Person to Trust God

Paul says for people to imitate him as he imitates Christ. However, Paul also says that he wants to bring people to God.[15] The key for the coach is to help the coachee to trust in the Holy Spirit. If the coachee lacks wisdom, only God can truly supply the needed insight. The coach's job is to help the coachee find God's unlimited wisdom.[16]

Many pastors lack a simple faith in God. I coach pastors to follow this line of thinking: "God says it. I believe it. That settles it." We need to go back to standing on the promises of God and simply obey Him.

The coachee needs to emulate Jesus, the one we profess to follow. If he does not know what the best thing is to do in a given situation, the coachee can ask himself, "What would Jesus do."

The coach cannot always be at the coachee's side, but God can.

Help the coachee to see God at work in his life and in his church. The faith of many pastors weaken as they continue in their service as pastors. The coach's job is to help him or her build strong faith in God and to be on fire for Him.

Joseph never felt that God loved him. He grew up in a very strict home where his father had little to do with him except in disciplining him. He could never please his father. Nearly every time his father spoke, he would rebuke him for something he had not done well.

Then Joseph became a Christian. He felt that God was like his father, always rebuking him for not being a good Christian. He tried hard to please his Heavenly Father, but always fell short of the mark. As a pastor, he worked hard at performing his duties, but never felt that God loved him or accepted him.

My job as a coach was to help Joseph to see and feel God's love for him. Over time, Joseph's life was totally changed. His marriage and family were transformed. And yes, his pastoring is so much more effective now.

Coaching is Church to Church

Coaching does not have to be just pastor to pastor but can also be church to church.

The coach should let the whole church know that he is coaching. Then he should try to mobilize the members to help in the coaching process. There are many things that the pastor cannot do, and he has to realize that the members have a key role in helping.

The more we can get the members involved in coaching, the better. The more the members catch what the pastor is talking about, the easier it is to change the church.

Paul is the pastor of a Baptist Church that has the Board of Deacons as the main decision-making body. Instead of going by himself to coach a church, he would often take some of his deacons with him and let them do the sharing with the coachee's church. Going with Paul opened up new possibilities for the deacons. They were able to envision how they could also help in the coaching process.

In the first chapter, I shared the story of Anna coaching Catherine.

I didn't mention, however, that besides coaching Catherine, Anna sent nine members of her own church to Catherine's church. They became members of Catherine's church and have brought a new atmosphere to that church. They are passionate but very ordinary people. But their lives are exemplary. They are influencing the rest of the church members in a great way.

It's amazing that one church would send members to another church to help that church. Yet, this is not the first time that Anna's church has done this:

- Four families were sent out to help another church. After helping in one church for two years, they are now in another church as members to help out.
- Anna is coaching another church, and she encouraged another family from her church to go to this other church to become members and help out.
- Anna's church also sent youth workers to another church to help them develop youth ministry.

This idea of sending out members to help another church is quite unique but very effective, and Anna is now trying to mobilize more people to do this.

Coaching Is Helping Pastors of Small Churches

Churches with the greatest need are the small churches. The church overall is continuously featuring the mega-churches as the successful ones. Pastors from the mega-churches are the featured speakers at seminars and conferences. Christian magazines and newspapers feature them and organizations look to them as superstars. By doing this, we are in effect saying to these small churches that they are not that great.

Small churches comprise the great majority of churches in the world. Even in Korea, the land of mega churches, the majority of churches are very small. Most Korean pastors are very faithful and love the Lord, but they are not growing big churches.

And the fact is that most small churches will continue to be small. In fact, there is no indication that God wants all churches to be mega-churches . Over 80% of churches in the world are less than 100 people, so just maybe it's God's norm for a church to average between 50-80 people. The fact is that small churches are normal. We are not saying that big churches are wrong, but we are also not saying that they are the "norm."

Most pastors became pastors because they love God and desire to love His people. The reality is that in a small church, this can happen most effectively. In fact to become larger than 80 people, the pastor will need to become more administrative, and he may need a skill he does not have. Large churches need entrepreneurs, and very few pastors are like this.

If it's the norm for the church to be small, we do not have to stress if we don't grow larger. So what we must turn our attention to is "multiplication."

The coach's role is to help the coachee to multiply. All multiplication starts with multiplying in the lives of others. As we reach out to others and disciple them, we are helping the multiplication process to take place. Such multiplication could lead to the multiplying of churches. To multiply the church we need to first multiply ourselves in the lives of others.

Once the pastor has begun to coach the members and help them to reproduce, then the church will be ready to multiply into additional churches.

One church in Japan became outward looking as it caught a vision for helping other pastors through coaching. This church decided to plant ten churches within five years and already has more than ten new church-planting teams ready to launch. The church is simply waiting to announce the official starting of this new vision of church planting.

Another church that has grown slowly felt God giving them a vision of planting forty churches in ten years. This church has already started a few simple churches, all initiated and led by lay leaders.

There are quite a few other churches in the coaching networks that are now moving in the same direction. In the next few years, we may see not only a coaching network, but the birth of a church planting movement.

Chapter Five

Friendship-based Coaching by Joel Comiskey

My coach never spends time with me," the hurting leader confessed. "He administrates me, directs me, and even continues to exemplify small group leadership. But what I really want is a friend. I want someone to take me out for coffee, to occasionally 'hang out with.'"

As a researcher, I've spent many hours trying to discover the principles behind effective coaching. I've searched for secret formulas and hidden mysteries. When I finally discovered the principle of friendship, I was embarrassed by its simplicity. I felt like the famous German theologian who boiled down all his years of research into one phrase: "Jesus loves me this I know for the Bible tells me so."

Friendship. We often overlook this simple, yet powerful principle. Jesus, the ultimate coach, revealed this simple KEY in the book of John when He said to His disciples, "I no longer call you servants, because a servant does not know his master's business. Instead, I have called you friends, for everything that I learned from my Father I have made known to you" (John 15:15).

Jesus entered a friendship with twelve sinful human beings, whom He mentored for three years. He ate with them, camped out with them, and answered all their questions. The gospel writer, Mark, describes the calling of the twelve this way, "He appointed twelve—designating them apostles—that they might be with him. . . "(Mark 3:14).

Sharing the Journey

Jesus didn't simply teach His disciples about prayer. Rather, He asked them to accompany Him to prayer meetings. He allowed His disciples to see Him praying. When the disciples finally asked

Him what He was doing, He seized upon the opportunity to teach them about prayer (Luke 11:1-4). The same is true with evangelism. Jesus evangelized people in the presence of His disciples and then instructed them afterwards. He took advantage of real life situations to carefully explain complex doctrinal issues (e.g., rich young ruler in Matthew 19:23).

The best teaching, in fact, is the natural type that occurs spontaneously. In these times, the leader coaches through a caring friendship. Everything else will flow naturally.

The word journey truly depicts the relationship between coach and pastors. It's a journey. It's a get-to-know you lifestyle that continues long-term. Small talk, joking, and other activities contribute to the overall journey of getting to know the pastor. I never count it wasted time when I'm talking small talk with my coachees. I try to start my conversations by asking about family and spiritual issues.

Coaching is a friendship journey. The coach and pastors walk together on a friendship journey, and the journey grows through relational friendship—or it will break down altogether. Laughter, love, and good will are key elements in the coaching journey.

Friendship and respect are the glue that holds the relationship together. If a pastor is constantly asking, "What am I getting out of this?" or "Is this coach worth the price I'm paying?" the relationship is destined to fail.

Part of the reason that it's a journey is because the coach himself is on a journey. He or she is experiencing change in all areas of life. This change will be reflected in the coaching sessions. The coach and pastor will be different the next day.

He might have read information from a book one day that related to the experiences of that time period. Today that same information will apply to a different context. Who I am as a coach today is different than who I will be tomorrow. As I grow as a person, I might emphasize certain things over others. There have been times when I've strongly emphasized evangelism. Other times I've focused on training or coaching. It just depends on what God is showing me or the set of circumstances I'm facing in my own ministry.

Relational Authority that Comes from Friendship

Karen Hurston, who grew up in David Yonggi Cho's church, tells the story of two cell leaders, one a polished, talented leader who couldn't grow his cell group, and the other, a bumbling, weak leader whose group was overflowing. The difference? The latter was involved in the lives of the members, while the former only arrived to lead a good meeting. It's all about relationships.[17] This lesson applies directly to coaches and coachees.

Greg Popovich coaches the San Antonio Spurs, an NBA team that has won the NBA championship four times under Popovich's coaching. One reason the players respect Popovich is because he's personal and has great people skills. Popovich has won his players' loyalty by getting to know them off the court. Point guard Tony Parker says, "It feels like a little family here." Veteran guard Brent Barry says, "He has the pulse of the team." Egan says, "He really connects with the players." [18]

Popovich not only excels in coaching techniques but also in getting to know his players "like a family." He commands the respect of his players because of the relational authority he has established.

Relational authority that comes through friendship is a type of authority that a coach can continually improve because it's based on his or her relationships, rather than position, knowledge, or spirituality. The coach can grow in relational authority by becoming friends with the leader. Knowledge, skill training, problem solving, group dynamics, and other techniques can play an important role in a coach's success. But what a coachee really needs is someone to bear the burden, to share the journey, to serve as a sounding board.

I'm increasingly aware that the most important thing I can do is to allow people to see the real me and develop a deep relationship as a result.

One pastor I was coaching called me during the week to discuss a particular problem he had in his own life group the night before. His pregnant wife was ready to quit the ministry because a piece of furniture was damaged due to an out-of-control child. This pastor felt the liberty to call because we had established a friendship.

Granted, becoming a friend can be difficult because of the time and space constraints to initiating and maintaining a friendship, but as much as possible, it should be a top priority of every coach.

More than Results

I coached one pastor who saw our relationship as a tit-for-tat experiment with getting a certain financial benefit. He was always thinking dollars and cents. He prided himself in his black and white approach to life, and I felt his critical spirit. He wanted to measure whether my time with him was worthwhile or not.

If a pastor is only focused on the money and what he's getting out of it, it will place undo pressure upon the coaching relationship. Within the friendship journey between coach and coachee, moments will surface in which teaching is at a premium, and the coach can pour new information into the leader's life. Other moments are more mundane in which it seems like nothing is happening. Again, it's all about of the coaching journey.

Pastor Jim Corley and I are good friends. I coached Jim for three years, flying to Arizona each month. During each of my trips, we spent a day and a half together. Our coaching time involved small talk, serious discussions, teaching, enjoying a meal together, meeting with staff and leaders, and drinking lots of coffee. I discovered that my coaching grew in authority as I hung out with Jim and developed a friendship with him.

Friendship makes it easy to coach a pastor. Without friendship the journey becomes fragmented and difficult. Friendship pulls it all together. Fun, laughter, and asking about kids are all part of the coaching dynamic. Apart from this, the coaching can grow informal and unproductive.

Some pastors only want to talk business—yet business is only part of the coaching relationship. Friendship and being on a journey are part of the overall package.

I do think that a pastor should expect results. The coach should realize that he or she is suppose to offer quality support at all times and should be available to give that support. However, coaching is more than results. Relational friendship is the glue that holds it together.

The coach's tendency is to want to get lots done. This is a reasonable desire, but it's just as important to leave enough time available to get to know the leader. If everything is business, the coach won't be able to speak into the coachee's life at a deeper level.

Ebbs and Flows

Picture a rushing brook and a small pond into which the brook flows. There are times when the intensity of the coaching experience is at maximum level as the water in a rushing brook. Other times it seems that nothing is happening as the water in the tranquil pond. The coach continues to go over the same plays, but nothing exciting seems to happen.

At times there will be more illumination than at other times. There will be weeks where nothing gels, and there's nothing new. Those weeks will be shadowed by weeks of great excitement and illumination. Changes often come in spurts.

Sometimes the individual being coached might report great statistics, while at other times, he can only see the valley. I wrote in my journal about one pastor I coached, "I've been on a high right after we made the cell goal, but now I'm on a low—only about four months later! Why? Several key leaders have left and the pastor is feeling discouraged."

This is the ebb and flow of cell ministry. It's natural and normal and part of the process. On those weeks when insights abound and great strides are made, the coach might work double time. He might make up for the lulls of the coming weeks and months.

Yes, the coach must labor diligently to make sure those ebbs and flows are natural and not the result of his incompetence or lack of direction, but the coach does need to expect that they will occur.

Confidentiality

A key element of the friendship journey is assurance of confidentiality. The coachee must be assured that everything shared stays between him and the coach.

The coach must be crystal clear about this. Just remember that the coachee is sharing his soul with you, the coach. He's opening a part of his very being. Just like a trained counselor, the coach shouldn't share confidential information he has received from anyone else, and he shouldn't disclose information shared by the coachee. *Leader as Coach* says,

> The temptation to bring people into your confidence by sharing insider information or criticizing others can be very compelling. The short term gain is often a feeling of special trust with your confidant. But when you share confidences or criticisms with people, you ultimately erode their willingness to share their vulnerability, weaknesses, and concerns with you.[19]

The coaching environment is the place where the coachee can share the truth, and that environment needs to be secure. At times it becomes tricky because the coach wants to give everything he knows to the coachee, and it might seem beneficial to talk about the experiences of another coachee.

When coaching churches, if I do share illustrations of other churches, it's only on a very positive level, esteeming what another pastor is doing for the sake of encouragement, while not going into details. In fact, when I speak positively of other coachees, the one I'm coaching realizes I'll honor him or her in front of other pastors as well.

Even in tough times, the coach's commitment is never to talk badly about someone else. Stephen Covey has emphasized the fact that when someone talks badly about someone else, the person with whom he's talking will feel insecure, knowing that he might be the subject of future gossip. Avoid gossip and stay clean.

Practical Suggestions

Let's get practical. How can you, the coach, befriend those small group leaders under your care? Here are a few suggestions:

- Invite the leader to your home, if it's possible. Let him or her see your family, your dog, your life.
- Go out for coffee with the person.
- Start the coaching call by asking about family, the weather, or any other personal detail.
- Send the leader a birthday card, a get well note, or a spontaneous "off the wall" humorous letter.
- Invite the leader to play sports with you, or some other normal life activity.
- Pray daily for the person (which will solidify your spiritual friendship).

Everyone can be a friend.

You probably knew the principle of friendship all along. If not, I'd encourage you to start now to build a sincere, caring relationship with those who you're coaching. Like me, you'll discover how such a simple truth can have a powerful impact on people's lives.

Chapter Six

Ordinary Pastors Can Coach
by Ben Wong

The idea of coaching pastors and churches is still relatively new. In the Asian context, no one would consider coaching a pastor or a church unless being trained and certified by an organization that specialises in helping churches and training coaches (e.g. Natural Church Development, CoachNet International Ministries, Church-Coaching Solutions, etc.)

Even then, there are very few such people around. Credibility is a major issue. A pastor might think, "If someone has not 'successfully' pastored a church, how can he coach me?" After all, can someone who does not know how to play basketball, coach a basketball player? Can someone who is not a doctor train future doctors?

Many years ago, I gathered a group of pastors who were willing to coach and also a group of pastors who wanted to be coached. I explain to them that I would pair them off – people wanting to be coached with those who were willing to coach. I told them that they could always change later on.

After a few months, we discovered that the coaching did not take off. As we evaluated why, we discovered that the reason is that it's very hard for Chinese to say to someone, "I am now your coach." We realized it was also hard for many Chinese to acknowledge another peer as a coach. The whole experiment of developing more coaches was a big flop. It never happened!

I came to realize that in order for ordinary pastors to coach other pastors in the Asian culture, we needed to build a new culture. We needed a culture in which coaching was not imagined a big deal. We needed to help people understand that coaching is not just for the professionals and highly qualified people. In fact, a person does not need to be formally trained and certified as a coach in order to coach.

People Helpers

Gary Collins wrote a book called *How to be a People Helper*, in which he insists that counseling is not just for specially trained people but also for ordinary Christians. He believes counseling is a key part of what it means to be the church, the loving community of God's people. Some may choose to call it "people helping" but in essence, Collins argues, it is "counseling." He says:

> Many people can be effective people helpers even though they have little or no training. Other terms to describe this is caregiving, encouragement, meeting needs, reaching out to, giving support, or friend to friend helping.
>
> Counseling can and must be a vital part of the church. People have problems and caring and helping people with their problems is a basic part of the community living of the church. This caring is not the sole task of the pastor or the trained professional counselors but the normal Christian also must be responsible for the meeting of needs of others. [20]

Every Christian should be involved in people helping. Some people have special expertise in this area, but every Christian has opportunities to help people in other areas of daily life. In fact, many people prefer to talk to a non-professional about challenging issues. These "ordinary" Christians may have little or no training, but they can make a significant impact nevertheless.

We all know that evangelism is not only for the trained church worker or gifted evangelists but for every person in the church. Caring for the needy is not only the work of trained social workers, but for everyone who follows Jesus and is willing to love "his neighbor." [21]

We are not discrediting the ones who are specially trained to counsel others or who are gifted and trained to be evangelists. But we are saying that everyone needs to be engaged in the work of counseling and evangelism at levels that are within their ability.

In the same way, every pastor needs to be engaged in the work of coaching. And if it's necessary, why not just call it "pastor helping." Many pastors can be effectively helping other pastors with little or no training. The bottom line is that you do not need to be a trained coach to coach.

In fact, it is important for us to have a coaching movement that is not based on formal training and qualifications but is based on a heart's desire of wanting to help other pastors and then learning new things along the way. Collins writes:

> We should not assume that we learn to be effective people helpers solely by reading a book, any more than you can learn to play the piano or to swim by reading a book. People helping involves interaction with others. The best people helpers are those who practice their helping skills and who are involved in the lives of others. [22]

Coaching Networks

Over four years ago, I came up with the idea of a "Coaching Network." [23] I started the experiment in Kansai, a district in Japan while talking with two Kansai pastors over dinner. [24]

My idea was to gather struggling pastors with those who were willing to serve as coaches. I was willing to be the catalyst.

We decided to come together four times per year for a miniseminar, and I was willing to be the speaker in order to introduce the coaching concept. [25] In between the seminars, the coach would meet with the coachees assigned to him or her, talking about principles learned in the seminar and about life in general. The commitment was for a term of one year with the possibility of renewing that commitment afterwards.

Each pastor needed to sign an agreement, indicating that they were serious and willing to attend the seminars and receive coaching. We also wanted pastors to understand that they didn't have to pay a fee for the coaching. [26] The only obligation was for each pastor to reach out and help other pastors.

We started in the Kansai area in Japan with four pastors willing to be coaches. In exactly four years, the coaching network grew to twenty-six coaches and a total of over sixty churches involved. Moreover, there are now four coaching networks in Japan.

Christianity in Japan has been growing very slowly. In more than 150 years, Japan has less than 0.5% of the population in church. Everything happens slowly in church circles in Japan. However, the coaching networks have expanded so fast that it has shocked everyone.

Although there is no strategy to extend the network and there is no central administrative or planning body, God is leading in amazing ways.

The four regions that we have coaching networks operating are: Chubu Region, Kanto Region, Kansai Region, and Shikoku Region.

Area	Main Cities
1. Kanto	Tokyo, Yokohama
2. Kansai	Osaka, Kobe
3. Chubu	Nagoya
4. Shikoku Island	

However, now four pastors in the Shikoku coaching network come from a prefecture called Yamaguchi , which is in the farthest southwest of Chugoku Region. One of these is a new coach in the Shikoku network.

These pastors are networking with many pastors in Yamaguchi, and they are excited to hear about the coaching network. It is quite far to travel to Shikoku, but they are keen to see this network come to Yamaguchi. So by the year's end, we hope to go there with the goal to start the Chugoku coaching network early next year.

In the southernmost region of Japan, Kyushu, pastors are interested in cell churches through the many testimonies of lives and churches that have been dramatically transformed through the coaching network. They have invited these "pastor coaches" to come to their churches to share their stories.

The exciting thing is that the rapid growth of the coaching network has not been through any human push, but rather through the testimonies of pastors and churches that have been dramatically changed through receiving coaching and the coaching of others.

For example, in 2007, the coaching network in Japan extended from Kansai (Osaka Area) to Kanto (Tokyo Area). John was the youngest of five coaches, and his church was also the smallest (less than fifty members). Like all the other coaches, he had never been a coach, but he was willing to try.

As he was relatively young by Japanese standards and his church was small, he was assigned to coach only one pastor named George, along with an older and more experienced pastor. [27] John did a great job coaching George, who had been so discouraged that he wanted to quit the ministry because of denominational control and betrayal by his own members. In one of those desperate moments, George called John, and John drove 1.5 hours to be with George through his dark night of the soul.

George later commented, "If I didn't have the coaching relationship of John who truly became my friend, I would have resigned and wouldn't be involved in ministry today." John coached so well that he was assigned another pastor to coach after one year.

Another example is Pastor Peter who was in his 60's and had pastored the same church for over twenty years. The church had grown to twenty members in twenty years, even though Peter had tried hard to grow his church.

Peter said to his wife, "Is this how I will end my pastoral life? Will our church ever change?" As it happened, Peter joined the coaching network and discovered that his church was far too dependent on him alone. He began to share with his church members about his new discoveries, and the atmosphere of the church changed. The pastor and members visited a cell church in the coaching network and started cell groups among members who were between sixty and ninety years old.

Since then, they have reached out to their community, people have come to know Jesus through the cells, and the church has built a solid relationship with the local community.

The local TV station heard about the church's ministry, came to the church to find out what was happening, and even made a broadcast about the church's new life and focus. This church became an encouragement to other churches in the area, proving that even a small church with aging members in a small town can have a powerful impact in the community.

Peter said, "If I were not coached, I would not have known what to do and would continue to be in despair. But now because of coaching, we are able to make and see powerful changes." Now Pastor Peter and even the church members want to coach and serve the churches in the neighboring town. Freely they have received, and now they want to freely give.

There are many stories like this from just four short years of implementing the coaching network in Japan. There are now over sixty churches involved in the four coaching networks. All of them are joined together through word of mouth and the testimonies of those being coached. We have testimonies of pastors' marriages being saved from the brink of divorce due to neglect. We've seen churches dramatically turned around while others have changed more gradually. Nearly every pastor has benefitted from the coaching, and as a result, their churches are now healthier and stronger.

There are now twenty-six pastors who are coaching others. The exciting thing is that not one of them would have dreamed of being a coach before the coaching network started. Moreover, many of them were even struggling as pastors before they joined the coaching network, but now they are coaching others.

Matt joined the coaching network in Kansai in 2007 to receive coaching. He lives over four hours away in the Southern Island of Shikoku. Because there was a dearth of coaches, when he signed up, the coaches asked him to coach rather than receive. Their request surprised Matt, but he was willing to give it a try.

Since joining the network, he has experienced enormous change in his life and ministry. His family life has improved. As a typical Japanese pastor, his leadership both at home and in the church was very top down, but now it is relational rather than just hierarchical.

The church has also become much more relational. Matt used to be office bound, but now he visits and mentors his members and walks alongside of them in their daily lives. Many of his members have become great witnesses in their work place.

Being a coach has blessed Matt a lot! He is now coaching six other pastors and is often away from his church. This has become a great blessing to his church as more people have risen up and have taken responsibility. The church used to be a pastor-centered church, but now it is Christ-centered as they have stopped relying solely on their pastor. The church members also go with Matt as he coaches other churches.

Matt said, "What makes me excited about coaching is that I meet different people who share the same values. We become good friends and we influence each other. Moreover, the influence has been far greater than I could have imagined!"

The first pastor who Matt coached was from the same denomination. It's thrilling to know that this same pastor is now the head of that denomination and is now promoting cell church, even though he used to resist it.

One elderly pastor, Henry (not his real name), was well respected, having pastored his church for over 40 years. The church is considered a model church in Japanese standards. Henry was also one of the original coaches when we started the first coaching network in Japan.

God stirred Henry's heart to see the potential of a coaching network that would bless many pastors in Japan. He also saw that ordinary pastors could effectively coach other pastors. Henry decided to dedicate the rest of his life to building up a coaching network movement in Japan. He wants to fulfill the dream of "no lonely pastors."

Henry decided to hand over his church to a younger pastor. This type of handing over usually doesn't happen in Japan. Usually the senior man holds on to his leadership until he cannot do it any longer, and even then he reigns from behind the scenes. The handing over was actually a great success, and now Henry is dedicating all his time to the Japan coaching network.

Hong Kong Coaching Network

Two years ago, we started the same sort of coaching network in Hong Kong, and now we have nine coaches with a total of over forty churches involved. Again, the stories are touching!

I mentioned the story of the woman pastor, Anna, who had served God faithfully for over twenty years but was depressed and experiencing headaches every day because of the struggles in her church. Another female pastor, Catherine, connected with her and began to coach her in 2006. In 2007, Anna joined the coaching network, and Catherine continued to coach her.

Now Anna is a happy pastor, and her church has dramatically changed. The members are on fire for God and are in cell groups. There is new life in the church. In 2008, six new believers came to Christ and remained in their church (three times more than in the previous five years put together).

She now has a group of pastors she can share and learn together with. They can laugh, cry, and play together. Anna is no longer lonely. She has friends and fellow travelers on the journey of pastoral ministry. She now belongs to a family.

Anna is now ministering to her members and actually enjoys serving the Lord. Her church members contribute in the ministry and do not wait for Anna to do all the work.

The nine members from Catherine's church contributed as church members and helped the church transition into a cell church. The network is like a big family. When someone has a need, the rest are willing to contribute in any way they can.

The network has expanded at a pace that totally surprised all of us in the network! Already the pastors who have been coached are becoming assistant coaches. Their hearts are to pass on the blessings. In the past, many people joined the "cell church network" in Hong Kong to get something out of it, and when they received all they could, they stopped coming.

The coaching network is different in that those who are coached desire to one day coach others.

Coaching Must Produce Coaches

Through the coaching networks, we have been able to see ordinary pastors become coaches. Pastors who have never been trained to coach are now effective coaches. They learn to coach by coaching. As coaches get together during the quarterly mini-seminars to share what they are doing, they learn from one another. How exciting it is to see pastors who had no confidence stepping out and boldly blessing others.

But what is even more exciting is to see those coachees rise up and start coaching others.

Coaching pastors must become a movement in order to fulfill our dream of "No lonely pastors." A movie that came out in 2000 that inspired me in the formation of our coaching network was Paying it forward. The movie is about a 12-year-old schoolboy, Trevor, in Las Vegas, Nevada who was given a class project to complete by his social studies teacher. His task was to come up with a plan that would change the world through direct action.

On his way home from school later that day, Trevor noticed a homeless man, Jerry, and decided to make a difference in his life. Trevor then came up with a plan to "pay it forward" by doing a good deed for three people, who must in turn each do good deeds for three other people, creating a charitable pyramid scheme. Trevor's plan was to help Jerry by feeding and housing him so he could "get back on his feet." Trevor also helped two other people and they were to pay it forward to three others each.

Meanwhile, Chris, a journalist, was trying to find out why a total stranger gave him a brand new Jaguar car after Chris's old 1965 Ford Mustang was damaged in a car accident. The stranger's only explanation was that he was simply "paying it forward." When Chris asked him for more information, the man explained that, when he recently visited a hospital while his daughter was suffering an asthma attack, a gang member suffering from a stab wound actually took up a gun to force the doctors to examine the man's daughter before she collapsed, prompting Chris to begin his search again.

The story continues to unfold as more and more people begin to "pay it forward." Chris finally identified Trevor as the originator of "pay it forward," and conducted a recorded interview at the school.

Trevor explained his hopes for the concept, but voiced his concerns that people might have been too afraid to change their own lives in order to make the whole world a better place.

One day, Trevor came to the defense of a friend who was being attacked by bullies, and was trying to fight them off, although they were older and bigger. In the process, he was stabbed in the abdomen. Trevor was rushed to a hospital, where he died from the stabbing.

While his mother and friends were mourning his death, they saw a television news report about "pay it forward" and Trevor's death, and learned that the movement had grown nationwide. Venturing outside the house, they saw hundreds of people gathering in a vigil to pay their respects to Trevor, with yet more people arriving in a stream of vehicles visible in the distance as the movie ended.

In our own coaching network, we see more and more people "pay it forward." Take Joe, for example. He came into the coaching network to be coached. He was pastoring a small church with a twenty-seven year history. He felt inadequate and realized that he was very inward in temperament. In his struggle, he wondered if he should leave the church.

Through the coaching network, he has become more outgoing. He used to be non-relational, very serious and reluctant to take leadership in the church. However, he received comfort and encouragement from the other pastors. Through the encouragement and input from his coach, he decided to change.

Now he has a good relationship with his leaders. He has decided to get involved in people's lives. Even the relationship with his wife and children has greatly improved.

Previously, he had rivals but no friends. God has blessed him with many friends through the coaching network. By fellowshipping with these other pastors, his church has become livelier. The church now has eight cell groups, and 75% of all members are in cells. The members now have a desire to reach out. As a result, the church has grown significantly and last year experienced six baptisms. [28]

His church now wants to reach out to others. Its new vision is: "To become an instrument of God in these last days as we experience the love and forgiveness of Christ. Our church will serve Japan in partnership with other churches with the same values."

In 2009, two years into being coached, Joe became a coach when the Shikoku coaching network started. Now, one year later, one of the pastors he coached has become a coach. So now we have the fourth generation of pastors in the coaching network in Japan.

We Can Do It!

This is such an important fact that we want to proclaim it from the roof tops! We want to broadcast to the entire world! We want to tell you over and over again so that it will sink into your heart! This is what we want to tell you:

Ordinary Pastors Can Coach!

This is so exciting! It is only when we understand this that we can see coaching become a movement! But more than this:

Ordinary Coaches Can Reproduce Coaches!

Coaching by ordinary pastors can be very effective. You do not have to e trained in order to be a coach. Even an untrained coach can amazingly help change the lives of other pastors and churches!

Coaching Must Become a Movement!
Let's do it!

Chapter Seven

The Most Common Pitfalls of Coaching by Sammy Ray Scaggs

"Coaching is 90% attitude and 10% technique"
-Author Unknown

The goal of every adventure is to experience the mountain top or the peak. When we are given the privilege and opportunity to coach someone in life, we can see it as an adventure. Caution: If we maintain a focus only on the peak, we may miss dangerous pitfalls that can damage or even destroy a coaching relationship.

The real danger is if we are ignorant about the most common pitfalls. We may think we are coaching when we are not, and we are usually the last ones to realize it. Our attitude needs to embrace coaching as a challenge to reach the peak. In coaching, the "mountaintop" is to see the leader we are coaching reach his or her potential. It doesn't take professional training to see this. We want the coachees to realize that it is possible to experience personal transformation, reach their destiny potential, and to learn to both articulate and activate their God-dream. We want them to know that they are doing something of eternal significance that will change the world for many people who otherwise may have never experienced a touch from God. We reach the "peak" when they experience transformation!

Arriving at the peak of personal transformation is an exciting experience. Many years ago our family was in Colorado, and we took a short trip to the top of Pikes Peak Mountain, which has a summit elevation of 14,110 feet (4,301 meters). The day happened to be crystal clear – not a cloud in the sky. Our eight year old daughter

Sarah was sitting with me on an edge of the mountain. As we were dangling our legs over the ledge and looking out at the view, she said something I will never forget, "God did a good job, Dad!" I was speechless at the sight we were seeing and of hearing my thoughts articulated through my daughter's words. God had done a good job! It was spectacular and breath-taking all at the same time. A peak in coaching can be the same.

As we create a safe environment for the coachees to grow, vent, and dream out loud, God will often unlock dreams that have been stored up in their hearts from the time they were in their mother's womb (see Psalm 139:13-18).

Then years later, as we stay in touch with the coachee, we can see some of the fruits of their labor and once again experience "mountaintop moments" from coaching. A view from the peak allows us a vantage point to see things that we cannot see when we are in the valleys of life. We all know that life is not always living on mountain peaks, but we do desire to climb higher and higher so that we may see more clearly than from down below. Because we know that valleys of life do exist, let's spend some time looking at what some valley experiences can be in coaching other leaders.

Every new discipline and the skills needed to master it, including coaching, comes with both ups and downs, peaks and valleys, shortcuts and pitfalls. You see, a valley can be a pitfall which is an "unforeseen or unexpected difficulty or trap." Mountain climbing refers to this as a "pratfall" which is an "embarrassing or humiliating mistake." We all have made mistakes, and like most climbers we want to learn from those mistakes to become better and not bitter.

And, of course, as with any adventure there are peaks where we can have maximum breakthroughs with those we are coaching. But in this chapter we want to explore a couple of pitfalls of coaching that I have learned along the way that might be helpful to you as you step out and begin coaching others. You do not need professional coach training to learn these.

In fact, you may already know them, but we thought it might be helpful to review them if you are just starting out.

Pitfall #1: Not Having the Heart of a Coach

This shift must occur in your heart before you coach another. We all know that our ultimate model for coaching is Jesus. He is the Master Coach! He models everything we want to do in coaching, whether we are coaching in the business world or church-planting world. His style works everywhere. If we have the wrong heart attitude when coaching, it is just like trying to fix the electronic system of a car with a hammer.

We may try to look like we know what we are doing, but in the end it is an exercise in frustration for both the coach and the coachee. Damage can be done, and unfortunately we may be the last one to recognize it.

Jesus talked a lot about the attitudes of our heart. Here are some of the diseases that can affect our hearts. First of all there is the "religious heart". It looks good on the outside; but it is really empty, and there is no power. Coaching the way Jesus coached was for the express purpose of advancing the Kingdom. Look at His provocative words:

> Now Jesus turned to address his disciples, along with the crowd that had gathered with them. "The religion scholars and Pharisees are competent teachers in God's Law. You won't go wrong in following their teachings on Moses. But be careful about following them. They talk a good line, but they don't live it. They don't take it into their hearts and live it out in their behavior. It's all spit-and-polish veneer (Matthew 23:1-3 MES).

The objective is to see the person you are coaching liberated to go to the next level, whatever that may be in his or her life. We are coaching for transformation. Genuine transformation! But if we do not truly believe the person can be transformed and used by God, we won't communicate a life-transforming faith. If we don't believe the person has the potential to raise up a church that has not existed in the community, city, or nation, who will believe it? The coach must constantly depend on the Holy Spirit to do mighty things in the coachee.

It also takes faith, which opens the door of the second disease of the heart we must avoid – the "heart of unbelief." The heart of unbelief struggles with believing the potential of other people. This kind of heart always sees the glass half empty. It calls a partly cloudy day "cloudy" rather than "partly sunny." This type of person does not have an optimistic vein in his heart.

I must admit that I have been accused of being "overly optimistic," and it can get me in trouble at times. But when it comes to people and their potential, I will always err on believing in his or her potential. Why? Because that is exactly what Jesus did! He is the Master Coach, and He coached His disciples that way.

He coaches me this way every single day. How else could you and I have done what we have done through Christ, if it were not for His "Heart of Belief" in us? We need to follow His example and believe the best about people. And if someone is brought into our life who needs our coaching skills, we need to release our faith, not only in the One who created him or her, but also in the person we are coaching. Look at this individual through eyes of faith and ask Jesus to reveal to you the person's potential. And guess what will happen? Yes! God will show you what He sees in this person.

When you listen to their dreams, hopes, and aspirations, you can ask them open and powerful questions to unearth the gold that lies deep inside their hearts. As you do, watch God begin to transform them into what He had planned for their life all along. And guess what else happens? When you begin to exercise your faith and belief in them, they will begin to join you and believe both what God has called them to do and, more importantly, who they are in Christ!

The last heart disease to avoid is what I call the "kamikaze or banzai heart"! These two words were immortalized during World War II when the Japanese fought with all that they had to defend their nation. The kamikaze attack was best known for the kamikaze pilots who turned their planes into human guided missiles. Or what about the banzai charge when the soldier charged the enemy on foot with only a bayonet but no bullets left? Both come from the traditions of the Samurai and the Bushido codes, which were based on the values of loyalty and honor until death!

Personally, while I really like the values of loyalty and honor until death, I do not think kamikaze attacks or the banzai charge were really that effective. They are basically suicide tactics and make for great movie scenes, but in the end, both parties are usually destroyed. In coaching I have seen well meaning leaders "charge in" while attempting to do their best without being trained. Often they do more damage than good. So, I commend you for reading this book and pursuing the discipline of coaching with the heart of Jesus, the Master Coach!

Just realizing that you need some element of training means that you have a teachable heart and that will serve you all the days of your life. Why? Because all of us have something to learn. And when we ask the Holy Spirit to change our heart to be more and more like Jesus and to guide us to others who are great coaches, they can teach and model for us the heart of a coach. Then we will achieve greater and more effective levels in our ability to be biblical coaches for the Kingdom of God. This brings us to the next pitfall, which moves us from what I call the heart to the eyes.

Pitfall #2: Seeing the Person You Are Coaching with Limited Vision

Great coaches need eyes of faith. I have experienced this pitfall from someone who was supposed to be coaching me but instead decided to give me advice. It turned out to be the wrong advice.

When I was a young pastor, I felt the strong tendency to be a bi-vocational pastor. I wanted to both be active in the local church ministry as well as start some kind of business. But the leader who was training me made me feel conflicted, double-minded, and basically not committed to the Kingdom of God.

Nothing could have been farther from the truth! God simply had wired me differently than other leaders. I longed to be both in ministry and business since this was the call of God on my life. Currently I am living my dream by serving as a co-pastor in a local church as well as operating several businesses out of my home with great joy and fulfillment. Don't get me wrong. The leader who was trying to coach me was sincere, but he was sincerely wrong!

If he had listened to what I was telling him about how God had created me and my God-dream, he would have been able to release me into my destiny much earlier and saved me a lot of frustration as well. I have never forgotten that experience. So, when I look at someone that God has given me the privilege to coach and influence, I always try to help him or her to discover what mission, ministry, or destiny God has placed within the person's heart and then assist the person to uncover that God-dream. This takes faith on the part of the coach and the one being coached, but it is well worth the time and effort given.

Ara Parseghian says this about sports coaching, but it is true in life coaching as well: "A good coach will make his players see what they can be rather than what they are." This is exactly what Jesus modeled for us when He was coaching Simon who was becoming Peter, the Rock:

> When Jesus came to the region of Caesarea Philippi, he asked his disciples, "Who do people say that the Son of Man is?" "Well," they replied, "some say John the Baptist, some say Elijah, and others say Jeremiah or one of the other prophets." Then he asked them, "But who do you say I am?" Simon Peter answered, "You are the Messiah, the Son of the living God." Jesus replied, "You are blessed, Simon son of John, because my Father in heaven has revealed this to you. You did not learn this from any human being. Now I say to you that you are Peter (which means 'rock'), and upon this rock I will build my church, and all the powers of hell will not conquer it. And I will give you the keys of the Kingdom of Heaven (Matthew 16:13-19 NLT).

This experience transformed Peter forever. Jesus was not only prophetically revealing Peter's unique destiny, but He was speaking with faith over his life and believing in who and what Peter would become. When we look at those we are coaching through the eyes of faith, we begin to articulate their potential and accelerate God's working in their lives.

This moves us from the eyes to the hands. Here is the third pitfall.

Pitfall #3: Being a Dream Killer Rather Than a Dream Releaser

Great coaches activate the dreams in the leaders they coach. It takes only a moment to kill a dream and a lifetime to live it! Dreams, like relationships, are organic and can be attacked and destroyed very easily.

A thoughtless word spoken at the wrong time by someone of influence can prove fatal to a dream. A parent, teacher, employer, or leader can be well meaning and yet work in opposition to what God wants. Jesus shared His life mission and God-dream as the resurrected Christ. After revealing his mission, things got interesting:

> "From then on Jesus began to tell his disciples plainly that it was necessary for him to go to Jerusalem, and that he would suffer many terrible things at the hands of the elders, the leading priests, and the teachers of religious law. He would be killed, but on the third day he would be raised from the dead. But Peter took him aside and began to reprimand him for saying such things. "Heaven forbid, Lord," he said. "This will never happen to you!" Jesus turned to Peter and said, "Get away from me, Satan! You are a dangerous trap to me. You are seeing things merely from a human point of view, not from God's" (Matthew 16:21-23 NLT).

Peter goes from being encouraged for expressing his revelation of Jesus as the Christ to being rebuked for being used of the enemy. Jesus rebuked Peter because of his refusal to see the dream of Jesus as the resurrected Christ.

When the casual reader encounters this passage of Scripture the first time, he wonders why Jesus is so harsh. For me, the reason is clear. Satan is using a well-meaning person or leader to attack the God-dream of another. This happens all the time. I have heard more stories than I would like about well-meaning parents, pastors, and leaders who have thoughtlessly used words and their influence to destroy the dream of another. I believe it is in our sin nature.

When someone begins to talk about their dream, it threatens us without realizing it, and we do what one old fisherman told me once when I noticed his crab basket didn't have a lid on it. I asked him, "Why doesn't your basket have a lid? Aren't you afraid your crabs will climb out and get away?" His reply was simple and revealing to me. "The other crabs will see to it that no other crab climbs out." As I carefully watched the action I discovered that when one crab began to see freedom outside the basket and began to climb his way out, the other crabs would grab a hold of him and pull him back down into the basket and virtually no one got out! Our sin nature can at times cause us do the very same thing. And all the while we convince ourselves that we are doing a noble thing.

When someone has the courage to share his or her dream with others, our natural tendency is to become fearful and defensive. We often challenge the dreamer, make sarcastic comments, or even ridicule the dream before it is ever really articulated for the first time. The inspiration for this is Satan himself because he is quite aware of the danger of God-dreams, especially when it relates to church planting and what the impact will be on his kingdom of darkness. Those coaching church planters are doing what Reinhard Bonnke calls "Plundering Hell to Populate Heaven."

Our mission, if we decide to accept it, is to create an environment where the dreamers can dream out loud without retribution. We are called to not only listen and encourage the dreamer but also to ask questions that give the dreamer an opportunity to put words to his or her faith, imagination, and feelings that have been bottled up inside for quite sometime.

When we choose the route of becoming a "dream releaser," we are embarking on a course that will activate the one we are coaching to take action with their dreams and begin to move from the conceptual dream stage to the practical dream stage.

This moves us from the hands to the feet. Nothing works like a good positive kick in the pants to get the leader you are coaching going and to assist him or her to activate their dream. Once this happens the leader you are coaching will be off and running like never before!

Pitfall #4: Not Listening but "Telling" the Coachee What to Do

Great coaches listen, reflect, and ask questions, rather than doing all the talking. We covered this topic in the chapter on "Dream-based Coaching," but allow me make the point here that the Listening, Reflecting, and asking open and powerful Question cycle (LRQ Cycle) is ongoing in our coaching environment. I cannot count the times that leaders have told me they are coaching me only to discover that their definition of coaching is: "Do it the way I do it" and simply label it coaching.

What healthy leaders need today is another seasoned leader who is secure enough to *listen* and to resist the temptation to always *tell* the coachee what to do. When I really got a hold of this principle, it set me free from all kinds of pressure. For example, the pressure we experience to have to pretend that we have all of the correct answers. No one needs that pressure, right?

I discovered the life of a coach is fun and liberating. It is exciting to see and discover what lies beneath the surface of a young leader that the Holy Spirit has been at work in for years. It's wonderful to use the basic LRQ cycle (listening, reflecting, questioning) to reveal the God-dream stored up inside of them. It sounds easy I know, but it will require discipline to go from discipling, teaching, mentoring, advice-giving, and preaching to LRQ. Yet, it's not only possible but necessary, if we are going to really see dreams released within our sphere of influence.

Overcoming this pitfall means that we need to change the way we think. We need to use our mind to remember the LRQ cycle and break into a completely new paradigm and discipline, which will open doors for us and those we serve unlike anything we have ever seen before.

Pitfall #5: Trying to Do Something that Has Never Been Done for You

Great coaches need coaching. The way to learn how to coach someone else is not by reading it in a book or manual but to be coached by a healthy leader. Dr. Joseph Umidi is not only the founder and president of Life-forming Leadership Coaching (the largest Christian coach training ministry in the world), but he is my coach, friend, and partner in ministry. He has been coaching me for over ten years and is still my coach today.

I had experienced some very unhealthy leadership models prior to meeting Joseph. I was pretty skeptical that what I had hoped for and even read in my Bible was not being done in my generation. And when I was about to give up, God brought Joseph into my life. It all began with a simple presentation he gave at a leader's conference on healthy leadership styles verses toxic leadership styles. After hearing him, I was hooked.

We became fast friends and partners in ministry and before I knew it, I was living my dream of healthy leadership coaching. Not only was it possible, but it was replicable. He called it biblical coaching, but I did not care back then what he called it. I just wanted more and more of it, and I wanted to see it replicated in my life and ministry around the world. Why is it so important to me? My personal life was transformed. My marriage was transformed. My role as a father was transformed. My church and ministry were transformed, and the way I served leaders was transformed.

I am sharing all of this with you so that you will not overlook the fact that you need to be coached in life if you want to be an effective coach to others. It is a biblical principle. I call it the "order of father and son." I believe strongly in spiritual fathers and mothers and have discovered that even if you do not have natural parents who are strong believers in Christ, God can and will bring spiritual fathers and mothers into your life to guide and assist you in your walk with Christ. And if they are true spiritual fathers and mothers, they will coach you.

My spiritual father happens to be my father-in-law, Harold Buckwalter. He has been used by God to disciple me as believer, to mentor me as a leader, and to coach me as a spiritual father to care for others in a healthy way. It started over three decades ago when I was only eighteen years old but continues today, and I hope it never ends!

It makes me a better father (both naturally and spiritually), coach, pastor, and leader. It is the same for you. You can coach! But in order to coach, do not forget this all important principle, "You must be willing to be coached to become and continue to be a great coach!"

This moves us from our brain to our backside! We too need to be kicked in the pants to learn, grow, and continue to embrace our God-dream so we can be authentic dream releasers! We need to have SEA (support, encouragement, and accountability) to continue to grow and then authentically say to those we lead, "Follow me as I follow Christ!" If you do this, you both will experience transformation and see others transformed right before your eyes. This leads us to our sixth and final pitfall.

Pitfall #6: Coaching for Fun, Fad or Fascination

You must coach for transformation. We all have been around long enough to see things come and go in church, life, and culture. If coaching is a fad or it looks like fun, people get fascinated, but it will not last. It will pass quickly when something else that looks more fun or fascinating comes along. However, if we are being transformed by coaching and we then in turn are used of God to coach someone else and by His grace they are transformed, then it will become a life-long discipline that will bring us joy and fruit our entire lives!

This is the top of the peak you have been focused on all along. Just like climbing a mountain you run into challenges, lack of energy, and even some dangers along the way. You begin to wonder, "Whose idea was this to begin with?" Then you realize it was your idea. So you refocus on the task at hand and keep going. Then you finally arrive at the top of the peak. The view and the breeze are spectacular. That is what happens when we experience personal transformation or when we are used by God to coach someone else to experience personal transformation. Then, when we see the church born from our coaching or see it become healthy once again, we are looking at a view that exclaims like my eight-year-old daughter did on Pikes Peak: "God did a good job!" Because only God can transform a life! But He loves to use us in the process.

Why is coaching so effective? First, it releases the God-given ability to solve our own problems. Often the answer is within our reach if we simply have the guidance of someone to help us discover it.

Secondly, it is effective because our growth, which leads to transformation, is actually accelerated by the relationship, just like a coach and athlete who is training for the Olympics. The coach sees the natural raw talent of the athlete and then combines his or her experience and tools as a coach to assist the athlete to reach their potential that has been untapped up to this point.

The coach is not totally responsible and neither is the athlete but together a synergy is released that helps them achieve something that otherwise would not have been possible! That is what we want to see happen all over the world. We desire to see leaders released to plant and nurture thousands of healthy, life-giving churches who also release a self-replicating biblical coaching movement that releases others into their dreams!

One of my favorite examples of someone who has lived a life of continual transformation even in the midst of pitfalls is Joseph, son of Jacob. If you pick up your bible and read from Genesis Chapter 37 to the end of that book, you will see the way Joseph was able to navigate through the pitfalls of his life. He had both peaks and valleys during which he could have made other decisions. Yet, Joseph made the right decisions, and his testimony continues to influence countless lives today.

Joseph was a history maker because He allowed God to assist him to navigate around the pitfalls of his life and destiny. The pitfalls were used by God to give him an opportunity to make a choice and to develop his character. I love what the psalmist reveals to us about this process when he states:"Until the time came to fulfill his dreams, the Lord tested Joseph's character." (Psalm 105:19 NLT)

May God bless you as you climb the mountain, and may He bless others you coach through your life because of the decisions you make today! Remember, "Coaching is 90% attitude and 10% technique." You do not need to go to seminary to be a coach. You do not need professional training to be a coach. Anyone can coach if they have the heart of Jesus. You can coach! Only you have the power to change your heart and attitude so that it guides you in the right direction. As you do, you will see the effect of it immediately. If you want to learn more about coaching please contact our coach training team at Life-forming Leadership Coaching (www.lifeformingcoach. com) for more information. But you have enough information to coach now. Remember, you can do this! What are you waiting for? You can do it. *You Can Coach!*

Chapter Eight

Coaching by Focusing on the Essence by Ben Wong

Around the globe, there is a popular approach to coaching that is a bit different than what we are sharing. A pastor of a "very successful" church (usually a mega-church) decides that he wants to help other pastors learn from his church or his own experience as a "successful" pastor. Since many pastors want to learn from these "successful" pastors, they flock to his church.

Most of the coaching help comes from seminars, conferences, and resources that the successful churches can provide. They tell you what they have done, and how they did it. Then they try to teach you to do the same sort of things, so that you also can be successful. This results in the churches that are helped by the "successful" church, trying to imitate the model and reproduce the same model in their own context.

One of the pastors of a "successful" church described to me his philosophy as "McDonald's franchising. " He told me that every McDonald in the world is nearly the same because each one follows the McDonald's way. All the new restaurant owners must get training from McDonald's on how to do it their way.

Here is the problem: Many pastors have tried to copy these model churches, but very few have been successful in doing so. Church models, in fact, are very hard to copy.

The reality is that a model is basically how a pastor or church was able to successfully expand in a particular way for that particular place. Yet, there are fundamental problems with copying models:

• Over 80% of churches in the world are less than 100 people, which is hardly mega status. It is not easy for these smaller churches to copy how a mega church operates. The two are not the same.

• We shouldn't try to imitate a model. Not many pastors have successfully done this. There are some who have, but they are the exceptions rather than the rule.

• Imitating another model assumes that these models are universally applicable anywhere in the world. However, models are very cultural and often bound to a particular area or nation. That is why in missions, the key is to contextualise or indigenise. You need to make it appropriate for that culture.

• People are very different and unique. What works for one leader does not mean it will work for another leader in exactly the same way. By trying to copy someone else, we actually suppress unique individuality.

I am not saying that these wonderful churches with their incredible models are not important for us to learn from. We praise God for what He has done through them! They are an inspiration to us all. They provide us with a vision of what is possible. There are many things we can learn from them. However, we are not meant to imitate models. We can copy the principles that underpin the success of the model, but we must not try to copy the model.

We are not limited to learning from just one model. Rather, we should glean truths (principles) from all of them. The questions we should ask are: What are the principles behind these models that are common and universal? What are the key teachings of the Bible that these models are following? [29]

Seven Essences of the Church

In the year 2000, over 300 pastors from over 35 nations gathered in Indonesia for a Summit. We gathered to discuss issues that the churches faced at the time. At the summit, we discussed the issue of models. At that time there were divisions being caused by certain models that called for everyone to follow them fully. Even at the summit, some were asking others if they were following a particular model or not.[30] It was like the New Testament where people were saying "I follow Paul," and the others were saying "I follow Apollos."[31]

At the summit, I proposed that we do not focus on the models, but rather we should celebrate the wide variety of models. Since the model worked for someone in a big way, I suggested we honor the model, appreciate it, and learn from it. I suggested that we not emphasize models but determine the essence behind all these models that we could all agree with. I admitted that I wasn't sure if my suggestions would work, but that if everyone agreed on them, we would take the next few days to see if we could agree on the universal principles that were at work in all of the models.

Everyone thought it was a good idea, although many (including myself) thought that the probability of discovering common patterns was not high. To our surprise, we came up with seven essences (principles) that we could all agree on.

Over the last ten years, I have shared those seven essences with hundreds of pastors in many nations, and everyone agrees that these are key principles. These pastors are from churches that operate with various models—whether traditional churches, cell churches, G12 churches, or house churches. Yet, they all agree with the seven essences.

I am not saying that these are authoritatively the absolute Seven Essences of the Church of Jesus Christ. However, I've noticed that people generally agree with them, and I'm confident when using them to teach Christ's Church.

I am also not saying that you have to agree with these seven essences, but I am saying that we should not focus on replicating the models when we coach other pastors, but rather on the essences.[32] The great benefit in focusing on the essences is that the pastor's life and the lives of the members can be changed for the better. The other benefit is that they are not stuck with one particular model but look to draw from many models. Essences allow us to be creative!

Why We Need Coaches

I've mentioned that trying to imitate a model leads to frustration and eventual failure for most pastors. However, focusing on the essences (principles) has its difficulties as well.

Often, models can help us to change the way we do things in the church. Models present to us what we can do. They have an existing structure that we can copy. They have existing materials that we can use. They are examples that we can look at. "Come and see how we do it and how you can do the same."

- This is how a cell group is run.
- This is how you supervise a cell group.
- Here is our manual to train your cell leaders.
- This is the equipping track that we have produced so you can equip your members.
- This is how we run our worship team.
- This is how we run our youth department.
- This is how we operate our children ministry.
- The way to lead people to the Lord in the cell group is to do these things.

The difficulty in imitating a model is that the way things are done in one place may be different in another place. What works in a big city might not work in a rural location. Cultures vary from place to place and from nation to nation. Even the culture of every church is different. Some churches have a long history and have formed a culture that is hard to change.

Most of the model churches are mega-churches, and they have developed over the years a model that suits a large church. However, most of the churches that want to change are small churches. It is impossible to successfully implement a mega-church model in a church of only 50 people.

Take Solomon, for example. He is a pastor of a church of eighty people and has been doing cells in his church for five to six years. He has about 70% of his people in cell groups. His struggle is that the cell groups are like having another meeting for the members in the middle of the week. His members were used to having a mid-week Bible Study and prayer meeting on Wednesday for many years. So why do they need to have another meeting called "cell group"?

Solomon felt the cell meeting would be better because at least more people would be participating in this meeting, yet it was hard to convince the long-standing members of his church.

One day, Solomon discovered that he, as a pastor, was not building relationships with other members. He was a "job-oriented" pastor. As a responsible Asian pastor, he was working hard at doing all that he thought he needed to do, but even his own relationship with his wife was in a poor state.[33] He realised that he had caught the structure and activity of the cell church but not the value or the essence of the cell church.

A decisive change in this area of building relationships brought great change and blessing to the whole church in a very short time. The greatest blessing to Solomon was that his relationship with his wife and children went through a radical change, and he is now a happy person and pastor.

Like in the case of Solomon, what pastors and churches need is to understand the values or essences of a church and aim to change that first. We need to individualise or implement these essences into our own lives and then into the lives of our churches.

This is where coaching is most needed. Many pastors are not trained to transmit truth into the lives of their members. This is why so many pastors fail even in trying to imitate a model. They don't know how to make the needed adjustments to implement the truths that will change their personal lives and the lives of their churches.

To individualise and implement these essences, people need a coach to walk alongside them, to talk things through, to evaluate, to show by example, and to inspire.

I will briefly outline the seven essences that we all came up with in 2000 in Indonesia

I am using these principles in the mini-seminars in the coaching networks and am given great receptivity by all these pastors. [34] The way we are coaching is to help pastors understand and implement these essences in their churches.

Essence 1 – Relationship

Today, when people think of the church, they often think of going to a building. When someone says to you on Sunday morning, "Where are you going?" we often reply, "I am going to church." Of course, that is not correct! You cannot go to church. The church is not an organization, an institution, a building, or even a worship service. Rather, the church is the people of God.

You cannot go to church. The Bible never speaks of "going to church." Believers are the Church. Our lives are His temple. The New Testament reserves the word "ecclesia" to refer to the people of God.[35] It never uses this word to refer to a building of any sort. Where you are is where the Church is (the Church is more than one person. When you are at home, that is where the Church is. When you are at work, that is where the Church is. (The Church is more than one person. The preceding statements are not correct)

Ever since I was a young believer, I heard many people say, "If you want to understand the church, you must study the book of Ephesians, it is the Book of the Church." As a result, I have studied the book many times in order to understand the Church.

In my study of Ephesians, I discovered that the book as about relationship, love, and unity. When the New Testament teaches us about the church, it emphasizes relationship, love, and unity. Ephesians 2:14-15 says, "For he himself is our peace, who has made the two one and has destroyed the barrier, the dividing wall of hostility, by abolishing in his flesh the law with its commandments and regulations. His purpose was to create in himself one new man out of the two, thus making peace."

Look at these terms in this passage:
• Making peace
• Reconciliation
• Making "one new man"
• No more walls
• Destroying the barrier
• Make the two one
• Create in himself one new man

Do you get the message?

Jesus died, not just to save us individually, but to create a new humanity, a new society, one that does not have walls or hostility. It is a humanity that is completely united. And what is this new humanity?

It is the Church! . In fact, unity is what the church is all about. The Church is a living example to the world of the loving and united community that God has planned for mankind–what humanity is supposed to be like.

The chapter goes on to say that:
- We are members of the family of God [36]
- We are joined together to become God's temple [37]
- We are built together to be the dwelling place of God [38]

(Ephesians 4:3) "Make every effort to keep the unity of the Spirit through the bond of peace." The words are clear here. We are to "make every effort," "give it all we have," "make it our priority," and "put all of our energy into it." And what are we supposed to do?
- Pray?
- Read the Bible?
- Evangelize?

NO! To keep the unity! Do you get the message?
Then comes the seven "one" references:
- One body
- One spirit
- One hope
- One Lord
- One faith
- One baptism
- One God and Father of all

Ephesians then teaches three foundational relationships where love and unity are to be lived out:
- Husband and wife [39]
- Parents and children [40]
- Employer and employee [41]

These three relationships cover most people's everyday lives. However, these three areas of relationship are sometimes not considered by the church as important areas for ministry. If you are a good husband or father, you might not be appreciated or considered as serving God very well by the church. If you are an agent of unity and love at your secular job, you might not be considered as serving God by the church!

It is important to remember that church life is not limited to the confines of the church building. In fact the Early Church did not have any church buildings. In the Early Church, Christianity was the only religion on the planet that had no sacred objects, no sacred persons, and no sacred spaces. The Jews had their synagogues, and pagan religions had their temples, but the early Christians were the only religious people on earth who did not erect sacred buildings for their worship. The Christian faith was practised in homes, in courtyards, and along roadsides.

Church life and practice is not limited to what we do in the Sunday Service. The New Testament did not even require Sunday Services as we have them today.

The Church should be about relationship, love, and unity. The Church should be about our daily lives.

Many pastors are working hard and are lonely people with no close friends. There is something wrong with the ministry of pastors today. The Church supposed to be concerned about people and relationships. We urgently need to bring the Church back to the essences.

In my journey in coaching pastors and churches, I even discovered that many people do not know how to build relationships (especially with people who are close to them).[42]

Essence 2 – Participation

In a theological context, this essence is called the "priesthood of all believers" in the theological world. In other words, those who call themselves followers of Jesus Christ ought to "follow" Jesus. They need to follow the way of Jesus, which is the way of discipleship.

A person does not first become a believer and then later in his life a disciple. From day one, he is a follower of Jesus, and that means he is a disciple.

To follow Jesus means to be who Jesus wants us to be and to do what Jesus wants us to do . Everyone must participate in the will of God for his or her life. Jesus taught His disciples to pray that God's will be done in their lives.

Everyone must participate in the will of God for his or her life. Jesus taught His disciples to pray that God's will be done in their lives.

God is love, so they who follow Him must walk in love. Love is the nature of God. Those who love God must walk in love, which means loving God and others. Love is giving out rather than receiving. That is why Jesus says that anyone who wants to follow Him must give up himself and take up the cross (which is the symbol of sacrifice). We are called to a life of giving. In God's economy, to really get abundant life, you must give up your life.[43]

The devil is all about "self." In fact, one of his key deceptions is to make us self-centered. God's life is a life of giving and self-sacrifice. Jesus said that "You're far happier giving than getting." [44] It is the life that God designed for us. The life that is focused on oneself is miserable. Jesus' model for us is one of servanthood and giving away of his own life. Jesus said, "That is what the Son of Man has done: He came to serve, not be served—and then to give away his life in exchange for the many who are held hostage" (Matthew 20:28, Message).

Each follower of Jesus is designed by God to be a giver, a contributor, and a participator in God's will.

If everyone is a participant, then the participating can't be only in what we do in the church building or the church organization. Participation must be in what Jesus wants us to do in the world. Jesus says that we are the light of the world and the light is supposed to shine in the darkness of the world.

The first essence shows us the importance of our lives in our family and our workplace. This is the primary participation of the church of God through each Christian playing their part in these places.

Participating in the home has made a great impact in many of the pastors in the coaching networks both in Japan and Hong Kong.

Jeremy attended a coaching network in Japan, and his personal testimony touched many in this network.

The first impact of joining the coaching network was on his marriage. He acknowledged that he nearly lost his wife out of neglect. Their relationship was at an end. After the new realization of the importance of the home, he made an effort to relate to his wife, the result was an 180 turnaround. His wife saw hope in the marriage as the pastor husband suddenly caught the new essence of the church – being a pastor is all about life, not about the job.

Another pastor said, "I have been in the ministry for 40 years and I have never prioritized my family in my life. Understanding this essence has given me new life."

The church is to participate in the Kingdom of God in the world. The New Testament Church is a sending church. Jesus said, "As the Father has sent me, so I am sending you." [45] The way Jesus trained His disciples was to send them out to do things. The church is not meant to be a "coming church" but a "going church." It does not mean that we cannot gather together, but we gather in order that we may scatter to be God's light in the world. Our major participation as the people of God is in the world- – to see the Kingdom of God established in the world.

Many of the churches in the coaching network also become more outward when they catch the truth of participating in God's plan.

One of the coaching churches[46] has been sharing this essence with the church members. Now Japanese churches are famous for being very inward. Both the staff and the members began to see that many of the new contacts would not want to come back to this church location. So they begin to think of the possibility of bringing the church to the people instead of bringing people back to the church.

"Don't bring people to the church, but bring the church to the people." Some members took the church to a children's home, and the management at the home really appreciated it.

The pastor discovered that there was a house where ex-drug addicts lived together to support one another to stay off drugs. They followed the 12 steps, similar to Alcoholic Anonymous, and Step 2 told them to rely on a "higher being." There were 26 men who lived together– some have been there for several years. They didn't have much hope to stay off drugs if they left. The good news is that two of them came to know the Lord and are re-finding new hope in Jesus and His church. The thought came that they could start a "simple church" in the house.

Now the church has a new vision of starting ten new "simple churches" in the next 5 years. This is just amazing for a Japanese church. The members are so excited about this new vision. People have been praying and really want to do what God wants them to do. Once the new vision is launched, the target of ten new churches will be already reached.[47]

The other exciting thing about this church is that the senior pastor who was pastoring the church when the coaching network started has completely caught the vision of coaching and has handed over the church to a younger man after being there for many years. This type of handing over does not happen often in Japan. It's normal for a pastor not to retire until he cannot function anymore. Now this younger man is leading the church forward. The whole ethos of the church has changed from a rather inward church to a church that has most of the members participating in taking the church forward. They are taking the lead to see the Kingdom of God come wherever they are.

Essence 3 – Empowering

Since every member of the church should be a participant, then it is obvious that empowering them to participate must be very important for the church. People are not normally contributors. This is a consumer world, and most people who come to Jesus still expect to be a consumer Christians. People expect others in the church to give them something. People even use God in the same way--give me, give me, give me.

Because people are brought up as consumers and live in a consumer world, many churches have become consumer churches.

They provide all the services that the members want and don't empower the members to contribute. Many church members see the pastor as someone employed by the church to take care of the matters of the church and do the work of ministry in the church. That is why they expect the pastor to do most of the work.

However, every single member of the church is supposed to be a participator, and the job of the pastor and leaders is to empower them so that they can do the ministry. Christian Schwarz puts it this way:

> Leaders of growing churches concentrate on empowering other Christians for ministry. They do not use lay workers as "helpers" ... rather, the leader assists Christians to attain the spiritual potential God has for them. These pastors equip, support, motivate, and mentor individuals, enabling them to become all that God wants them to be. Rather than handling the bulk of church responsibilities on their own, they invest the majority of their time in discipleship, delegation, and multiplication. Thus the energy they expend can be multiplied indefinitely. [48]

We have already seen that Ephesians, the book that many see as a key book for our understanding of the church, is all about relationship, love, and unity —which all Christians can participate in. What does Ephesians say about leaders?

> "And His gifts were some to be apostles, some prophets, some evangelists, some pastors and teachers. His intention was the perfecting and the full equipping of the saints, [that they should do] the work of ministering toward building up Christ's body (the church)." [49]

God's intention for the church is that all the saints should be fully equipped so that they can do the work of the ministry in building up the church. The church today is very organizational, and so we even view these apostles, prophets, etc. as positions in the church.

As a result we miss the most important point of the whole passage: That all the saints should participate in building up the whole body of Christ.

To make this happen, God's people also need to be empowered. I am not sure that there are only five functions needed to fully equip all the saints, but God will provide the body with necessary equippers to do this.

"From him the whole body, joined and held together by every supporting ligament, grows and builds itself up in love, *as each part does its work*" (Ephesians 4:16).

This is also the way of Jesus! The major part of Jesus' ministry was in training the men that He selected. He concentrated on the twelve men, but without neglecting the seventy or the multitudes. Before He went to the cross, he prayed mainly for the twelve– that was His life work.

His ministry touched thousands, but He trained twelve men. He gave His life on the cross for millions, but during the three- and-a-half years of His ministry He gave His life uniquely to twelve men.

At the end, His instructions to His disciples were very clear, "Go make disciples of all nations." Go and do the same that I have done to you.

In my many years of coaching other pastors and in my connecting with many more pastors through the coaching network in the last four years, I've realized that discipling other believers is the weakest area of ministry of pastors.

In my previous chapter, I spoke of Matt who is coordinating the coaching network in Shikoku. Matt told me that what changed his church the most was that he now does not spend so much time in the office. As a typical Japanese pastor, he used to spend a lot of time in the church building and church office. That is where he did most of his pastoring.

Through understanding the principle of empowerment, he has come to understand that he needs to empower his members to be effective for Jesus where they are in their daily lives. He has begun to select a few to disciple, and he goes to where they are working to help them to be effective for Jesus there.

Now his members are beginning to bring changes for Jesus in their working environment. One teacher is starting to impact his school for Jesus. Matt says that he is now more meaningful as a pastor. He is now seeing his church making an impact in his district.

This leads us to a very important point in empowering: Do not empower your members to participate in the church building. Most pastors do some sort of training for their members. However, most of the training is done in the church building. Empowering cannot be a course or a series of teaching materials (although we can use all of them). Empowering our members must take place in their daily lives rather than in artificial environments.

Essence 4 – Focusing on Jesus

It is very basic that we recognise that Jesus is the head of the Church and not the senior pastor. In most churches, when something happens the members look up the pastor rather than going to God. It is obvious that the church is dependent on the pastor rather than dependent on Jesus.

How is our church dependent on Jesus? How will our church be different if Jesus or the Holy Spirit is taken away from our church? What will change? Will life go on? What are we doing now that is truly dependent on Jesus? What is it that we are into that we cannot do without Jesus?

That is why the best times are times when we are really at a loss without God, when we cannot do it by our own wisdom or our own resources. Of course it is even better when we realise we actually need God in everything we do.

Jesus said, "You're blessed when you're at the end of your rope. With less of you there is more of God and his rule." [50]

These were the first words Jesus spoke when He started preaching. What a great declaration! Most people would consider being at the end of one's rope as a bad thing, but not in the Kingdom of God. When I am weak, that is when He can be strong. That is why the Church should not run from hardships and tribulations. They make us more dependent on Him.

Jesus said, "I've told you all this so that trusting me, you will be unshakable and assured, deeply at peace. In this godless world you will continue to experience difficulties. But take heart! I've conquered the world ." [51]

Difficulties are part of the normal Christian life. Do not reject problems as enemies but welcome them as friends. They have come to help you and train you to cry out to God for help. When you have experienced that God is greater than all your circumstances, it will make you much stronger and fearless in life.

James says, "Consider it a sheer gift, friends, when tests and challenges come at you from all sides. You know that under pressure, your faith-life is forced into the open and shows its true colors. So don't try to get out of anything prematurely. Let it do its work so you become mature and well-developed, not deficient in any way."[52]

To put it in another way, do not always look for the easy way out of things. Do not just try to do what is possible and easy to do. God often brings hardships in our lives to make us stronger.

The key is "what would Jesus do"? "Focusing on Jesus" also means that we follow Him as an example. What Jesus would do often is very different than what the world would do or what we were taught to do. Remember the Church is to focus on following Jesus and not the world that we live in or we were brought up in.

Michael Frost and Alan Hirsh wrote a book entitled *ReJesus: A Wild Messiah for a Missional Church*. Notice their focus on Jesus in us:

> In order to follow Jesus you must also emulate Him, using His life as a pattern for your own. We call this emulation becoming a "little Jesus." When we call ourselves little Jesuses, we aren't claiming to be able to walk on water or die for the sins of the world. No, being a little Jesus means that we adopt the values embodied in Jesus' life and teaching. Only Jesus was able to feed thousands with small amounts of bread and fish, but as little Jesuses we can embrace the values of hospitality and generosity. We might not be able to preach to the multitudes, but we can commit to speaking the truth to lies. We can't die for anyone's sins, but we can embrace selflessness, sacrifice, and suffering.[53]

The church needs to train the members to be able to listen to the head who is Jesus. The best thing we can do is to empower our members to be directly connected to the head. What does the head want us to do? What would Jesus do in this circumstance?

The Church needs to realize that prayer is not a meeting, although we can have prayer meetings. Prayer is expressing our dependence on God. Prayer is not a ritual that we go through. Rather, it is truly trusting in Him. Do we truly look to Him and go ahead and do what He wants us to do regardless of circumstances?

- Jesus entrusted the future of the Church to His disciples who were weak failures-- hiding away in fear of suffering and persecution. Do we dare to entrust ministry to imperfect people?
- Jesus sent his disciples out, and He told them not to take a purse with them, asking them to totally trust God for their livelihood. Do we dare to go ahead with ministry without having the money to do so?
- Jesus would expose his disciples to dangerous situations. He took them into the middle of a storm in a boat. He brought them on a mission that meant persecution from others. Do we dare to be on the cutting edge where there may be danger and sacrifice?
- Jesus suffered as a result of what He did. He even went to the cross even though He knew the risk He was taking. Do we dare to take up the cross as well and follow Jesus?
- Jesus stood up against the authorities of His days when they were wrong. Do we dare to do what He did?
- Jesus did what was impossible for man. He healed the sick and drove out demons, etc. Do we dare to follow in His footsteps?

Essence 5 – Outreach and Multiplication

If the church is to focus on Jesus, then we need to be concerned with what Jesus is concerned about.

Jesus came for one reason and one reason alone--and that is to seek and save the lost. He started the Church for one reason and one reason alone--and that is to finish the work that He has started --and that is to seek and save the lost.[54]

The New Testament Church is different from the Old Testament Church (as illustrated by the diagram on the right.) In the OT, the Church is centralised in a nation (Israel), then in a city (Jerusalem), then in a temple, and then in the Holy of Holies (the presence of God). The world of nations will have to come to Israel to see the greatness of Jehovah God.

When Jesus died on the cross, the veil between the Holy of Holies and the Holy Place was torn in two. This cataclysmic event symbolizes that the presence of God is now everywhere. There is no longer a temple because now we are the temple of God. The motif of the Church has changed from a "coming" mode to a "going" mode. The relationship between the Church and the nations of the world is "go." The essence of what Jesus said to the disciples after his resurrection is: "Go into all the world!"

The command to go is the essence of the Great Commission of the Church. The Church should not have a "come" mentality. In the NT, there is no church building. But today, many churches are still in the OT mode of "coming" to the building to worship God. We can worship God anywhere since God is in our midst. Scripture tells us that where two or three are gathered in His name, He is in the midst. The church is the people of God wherever they are.

One day, I was teaching in a rather conservative Korean church about these essences of the Church, and the senior pastor spoke to me. He was in agreement with what I shared, and he said to me, "When you preach on Sunday morning, I do not want you to wear suit and tie. I want you to wear a T-shirt. This has never happened before in our church.[55] Maybe after this Sunday, I will be fired. I will interpret for you, and I will also wear a T-shirt."

So the pastor gave me a T-shirt that he had bought earlier, but had never worn. On Sunday, I turned up with this T-shirt, and the pastor also wore an identical one. As we stood before the congregation, they were all staring at us both in white T-shirts. The pastor asked the congregation if it was quite strange to see us in T-shirts, and everyone nodded their heads with their mouths open.

Then he got us to turn around. There in big letters on the back were the words, "DON'T GO TO CHURCH." It was a shocking message for everyone. Then down below these big words were small words, "BE THE CHURCH!"

Then I began my message on this topic!

You are the Church wherever you are-- so be the church!

We also have the Great Commandment: to love God and to love our neighbor. Someone asked Jesus, "Who is my neighbor?" To this question, Jesus gave a parable called the Good Samaritan. The gist of the message is that not the person who lives next door to me is my neighbor, but the person who is in need and who cannot help himself. If I am willing to reach out a helping hand, then I am a neighbor.

Loving our neighbor is not a choice that the Church can make. Rather, it is a commandment given in parallel to loving God.

We as the Church need to be a going Church that shines for Jesus wherever we are-- in our home, in our workplace, in the place where we live, and also to the needy of the society.

Essence 6 – Networking

We are all a part of the same body. We are a part of a whole. Jesus did not come to establish many churches but only one Church– and that is His Church.

One day I was preaching in my own church, Shepherd Community Church, for the Vision Sunday, which is the first Sunday of the year. This is when we share with the whole church the vision of our church for that year. As it was our Vision Sunday, it was a combined celebration of all our congregations and nearly everyone was to be there.

Before the Sunday arrived, some staff called me on the phone to ask me what the title of my sermon was because they wanted to prepare for the worship songs. My answer to them was, "You will find out on that day." On that morning, other people called me up to ask for the title, and I told them, "You will know later."

When I got to the hall where we were having the celebration, some people asked me for the title, but I said, "You will know." Finally, at the pre-celebration prayer time, I was asked again, and I said, "The title of my sermon is, 'God is not interested in Shepherd Community Church'." Obviously they thought I was joking, as I like to joke. They asked me, "Really? You are not joking?"

So I got up at sermon time and told the whole audience, "Today, the topic of my sermon is, 'God is not interested in Shepherd Community Church!'" Everybody laughed!

Then I said, "God is interested in His Church! God is interested in the city of Hong Kong! God is interested in the people of Hong Kong! God is interested in the churches in Hong Kong! But He is not interested in Shepherd Community Church. There is only one Church, and that is the Church of Jesus Christ! We are only significant if we are a part of the whole!"

To be honest, this value is the hardest for churches to understand. I have been involved in the networking of churches for over fifteen years, and it is a very lonely situation to be in. The "my church" mentality is so strong in the Christian world that networking together is a low priority for most pastors. I would even venture to say "the lowest." With most pastors, this ethos of being a "part of a whole" does not exist. It certainly is not a value of most seminaries.

However, in my opinion, this essence is number one for the Church of Jesus Christ to impact the world and to usher in the Kingdom of God. Without this, we cannot be strong, and there is no power in the church.

Recently, I have seen hope through the coaching networks. As people experience the unconditional giving of other churches, this essence begins to sink in to pastors.

After attending the coaching network for the first time, Abraham, a pastor who is in his 60's, shared this with everyone: "I have been a pastor and in the church circle for many years and have been to many conferences, seminars, and meetings. I have never, however, been to one like this where pastors are so open to share their lives with one another and where people come to give freely rather than to take. This is indeed a miracle for the Church of Jesus Christ. I never thought that this were possible. It is like living in a dream."

This pastor was in tears as he shared with us. He was full of joy.

I said to myself, "This is the beginning of a realisation of a dream. Even though it is just the beginning, I am filled with unspeakable joy."

Essence 7 – Adaptable Structures

Unfortunately, the worldwide Church of Jesus has become institutionalized. In the past, we loved organized church and institutionalized religion. People loved to live within the bounds of the rules of the church because it made them feel secure. But this is a thing of the past. We are now entering a new epoch of human history. All over the world, people are turning away from organized religion. The interest in institutional religion is going down fast.

In Japan, a Gallup Poll in 2006 discovered that only 30% of adults said that they had a religion and only 20% of youth had one. This was a surprise to many people because Japanese are known to be religious. They are either Buddhist or Shintoist. However, the poll tells us that Japanese are turning away from institutional religion as we know it.

Religion has lost its relevance to the people of this world, but Jesus is relevant. Do not make Christianity into a religion because Jesus never came to start a religion. Jesus came to bring us to God and to experience a new life. His coming enabled us to live in a new way.

Many churches have a rule for everything. Take membership. Many churches determine "responsible membership" by making a list of "guidelines for being a good member. Those guidelines end up becoming rules. What is a good cell leader? That is another good question that we often define by another list of rules.

Even spiritual things become structure. We need to pray for the sick. So how do we pray for the sick? First of all we need to work as a team, and the team needs to be united, so the team must first spend time praying together before we can pray for the sick. And then we need to put oil on the sick person. After a while, these become rules and structure.

It is not wrong to have structure, but structure is to serve us and not to control us. The Church is all about life and relationships. We are to be led by Jesus and the Holy Spirit. It is often hard to put the Holy Spirit into a structure. Structure is to be adaptable to the situation.

Models are good, but models are not there to rule over how we must do church. More and more the world is sick of institutions. The world is looking for relevance, and Jesus is relevant. We are not to be ruled by structure but guided by the radical mission of Jesus for a lost and needy world. Love God and love our neighbor cannot always be structured. The heart is the key for love. The willingness to lose ourselves and be concerned about service and sacrifice rather than be concerned about the style or structure of how it must be done – this is having an adaptable structure.

Conclusion

Coaching must go beyond imitating models. It must help the person to individualize and implement the essences of the church and by doing this create a new value and culture in the Church. Yet, we always must remember that a change in life is the key!

Making a Coaching Plan
by Joel Comiskey

Back in the 90s, I learned the benefits of belonging to the Automobile Club. Before traveling a long-distance by car, I would first ask an Automobile Club worker to map out the best route. Within minutes I knew exactly how to get to my destination. I could then enjoy the ride because my directions were clearly written down.

I can now do the same thing with the Internet, but the point is that knowing where to go provides peace of mind and a much better chance of actually getting there.

If someone fails to plan, he plans to fail. The writer of Proverbs said: "We should make plans ... counting on God to direct us" (Proverbs 16:14,TLB). The same writer goes on to say, "Any enterprise is built by wise planning, ... " (Proverbs 24:34,TLB).

I didn't make concrete plans with the first group of pastors I coached in 2001. I tried to figure out a plan along the way, but because I didn't know my destination, I couldn't give clear direction. During that same period, one of the pastors made an action plan on his own and gave it to me. I found myself looking at his plan a lot, as I prepared to coach him. His action plan helped me to guide him more effectively.

Make a Plan and Be Ready to Adjust

In 2003 I began a three-year coaching cycle with a new group of pastors. I soon realized that I had to adjust my plan for each pastor. Some pastors, for example, needed to move much more slowly. Like children, they were learning to walk. Others wanted to run. As I got to know each of them, I adjusted the plan accordingly.

Today, I no longer coach an entire group of pastors over a long period of time. Pastors come and go in and out of my coaching ministry, and I only require a six-month commitment. Some pastors come in with a high-level of knowledge about cell ministry and others with very little. Now I need to include even more flexibility in the coaching plan.

Sometimes the action plan is more internal (for my sake) while at other times, I lay it out with the pastor and we work on it together. Here are the basic steps I take when developing a plan for coaching pastors.

1. Begin with a foundation of knowledge

When I first started coaching, I assumed the pastors knew more than they actually did. I later discovered that many of them lacked foundational concepts and principles about cell ministry.

I committed myself to make sure the pastors understood the basics and were growing in cell knowledge. My motto is: The more knowledge, the better. I reject the idea that less knowledge is good, or that because pastors don't always implement what they know, it's okay to give them less.

Granted, we can exaggerate knowledge way out of proportion. Many pastors are filled with knowledge but don't know how to apply it. Yet, lack of knowledge is no solution either.

Coaching in reality is helping the pastor to practice the knowledge. To help them do this, a coach first needs to make sure the knowledge is there.

One great source of training is reading books. Peter Wagner said, "One of the very best ways to renew the mind is to read, read, read. Few leaders who do not read will ever get to the cutting edge." [56] I encourage pastors to read cell literature in-between our coaching meetings.

Some pastors prefer not to do this. They would rather have me focus 100% on their particular church situation, and because I'm their servant, I readily agree. However, if they do agree to my general plan, we start a reading schedule. Most agree to read one book per month, but some want to read two books per month. I point them to a list of cell church books I want them to read in the order I suggest they read them:

http://joelcomiskeygroup.com/articles/churchLeaders cellreadinglistbibliography.htm

Even if the pastor has read the book previously, I encourage him or her to read it again. A pastor can read too little but not too much.

During our coaching calls together, I'll ask the following questions about the book:

1. What was the author trying to say in the book? What was his or her objective in writing the book?
2. What were the strong points?
3. What were the weak points?
4. What lessons did you learn? How were you changed as a result of reading the book? What will you now do differently as a result of reading the book?

Most are already self-motivated, so the reading gives them keen insight in cell ministry.

Beyond the general book knowledge, I like the pastors to know what I teach in my cell seminars, so I give them my PowerPoint lessons. I ask the pastor to go over one PowerPoint lesson before the phone call, and then I take five minutes to answer any questions. I don't take a lot of time on this because I want to enter into the specific needs of the pastor, but again, I think it's important to establish a foundation of knowledge.

2. Build a Case Study of Pastor and Church

The phrase "case study" simply refers to a document that includes everything you know about the pastor and the church. This information might come through observation, the church's website, documents the pastor sends you, or what you hear the pastor saying during the coaching time. You will be adding to this case study throughout the time you coach the pastor.

If I'm talking to the pastor by telephone, I will have my notebook computer open while talking. I write things down in the case study as the pastor is talking. After the coaching session, I write down what I've learned.

The coach can't make wise suggestions and assessments without information about the coachee. As the coach analyzes the church, new insight will come to mind. Write the questions down you want to ask the pastor before each coaching session.

As you develop a case study, you'll have a running commentary on the life and ministry of the leader you're coaching. Some important factors are:

Who the Pastor Is

I ask the pastor about his family, marriage, and back ground. My goal is to discover as much information as possible. If the pastor has taken the DISC personality test, Strength Finder, or any other personality test, I ask him to send the results to me. Sometimes I recommend certain tests, like ProScan.[57]

History and Background of the Church

This includes when the church started, the number of pastors who have served, the main philosophy of the church (e.g., Bible focus, worship focus, etc.), some of the major high points and low points in the church's history, times of growth and decline, and all information the pastor can give to describe the church's background.

The Community and Cultural Context

What type of ethnicity surrounds the church and attends the church? Are the people rich or poor, transient or stable? A lot of this information can be obtained on the Internet. For example, in the U.S., by placing my zip code in a Google search, I can discover more information than I could ever need about race, ancestry, education, income, social status, population, lifestyle, and more. I can expand my search to include other zip codes of connecting cities.

If you have a chance to visit the community where the church is located, write down what you find and experience.

Attempts at Cell Ministry

Cho once said that a person has to fail three times at cell ministry to get it right. Find out what attempts have been made. Try to discover why the church failed in their previous attempts. It's important for the coach to know what the pastor has done wrong to help him or her avoid similar future mistakes.

3. Develop a Concrete Church Action Plan

As you talk to the pastor and understand where he wants to go, write down his future vision. World-class athletes frequently envision the final act of their events in their minds before it actually happens. They go through the event twice, once in their mind—a future perfect way of thinking, and then when it actually happens. And they make decisions in the present based on that envisioned reality.

With the information you've received from the pastor, picture the final state of the church before the transition or planting actually begins. Write down the situation as it is right now and then what the pastor dreams it will be in the future.

As the coach, you can dream about where you'd like to see the pastor go, but ultimately the concrete action plan has to come from the pastor himself. You will help the pastor work through the plan, but ultimately it needs to come from the pastor's heart. If not, it will be very difficult to get the pastor to do something he has not envisioned doing.

If you're coaching a pastor of a traditional church who wants to transition to the cell strategy, your plan will involve how to transition and goals in transitioning. If you are coaching a church planter, the steps will be much different. Let's look at different scenarios.

Transitioning

If the pastor is preparing to transition his church, begin with a plan to launch a pilot cell that the lead pastor will facilitate. After this pilot cell multiplies, plan to have the lead pastor coach the new leaders. Bill Beckham says: "The senior leader must model the community he is expecting everyone else to live in. If leaders don't have the time to live together in cell life, how can they expect members to do it?" [58]

Mistakes made in the prototype stage are more easily corrected before they spread throughout a group system. Key leaders are part of the process from the beginning, making it more likely they will actively support small group ministry. If the prototype group does not practice evangelism, neither will any of the resulting groups. If prototype group leaders do not model leadership development, neither will any of the resulting groups. [59]

When a passionate lead pastor breathes life into the very first group of people, the cell system is likely to start well. As you make your plan for transitioning, make sure you cover:

- Who will the pastor ask to be in the pilot cell? Before entering the lead pastor's model cell, all potential leaders must commit themselves in advance to leading their own cell group or being part of a new cell team.
- How long the pilot cell will last? I recommend between six months to one year.
- What kind of training will take place for those in the pilot group?
- How will that transition play out with the existing leadership structure (board, elders, etc.)?

Planting

The action plan in a church plant will be different. In my book, *Planting Churches that Reproduce* (CCS Publishing, 2009), I go into detail about each step. In summary, you'll want to guide the coachee through various stages of planting the church, asking the coachee for timetables for each stage:

- **Development of the Prayer Team.** Church planters need to be surrounded by prayer warriors who can lift them up in time of need. They need to ask people to commit to regular prayer, not just sporadic prayer.
- **Develop Vision and Values.** This is where I, the coach, will help them through reading, powerpoint teaching, etc. We will grow together in our coaching on the cell church philosophy.
- **Develop "Pre-Cells."** I encourage church planters to gather possible candidates for the first cell group by having pre-cells. One church planting couple, for example, considered offering a short term class on parenthood for those who are in the community. Others have used a series like Alpha to draw in newcomers.
- **Develop Pilot Cell Group.** This is when the church actually starts. This is the first church meeting, but it takes place in a home. I recommend having a few Christian couples, as well as those who have been gathered through the pre-cell activity.

• **Multiply Pilot Group.** When the pilot cell actually multiplies varies from six months to two years. Before the pilot group can multiply, the lead pastor needs to train those in the group. When the pilot group multiplies the lead pastor coaches the new cell leaders.

• **Begin Celebration Service.** When there are approximately three weekly cell groups, I recommend a monthly celebration service. Sunday evening is preferable. More frequent celebration services take place as more cells multiply. Social gatherings and prayer meetings can also serve as gathering points in the early days.

• **Continue to Build Infrastructure.** As the cells multiply, it's essential to fine-tune the coaching, training, multiplication, and prayer ministries.

• **Plant New Cell Churches.** The goal of a church is not just to be a church, but a movement of God, expressed as a global church-planting movement.

Training Track and Care System

A training track ultimately must come from the heart of the pastor and church. But many churches, in the process of developing their own materials, use the materials of others. My book, *Leadership Explosion* , explains what an equipping track is and the principles common in all training tracks. In the action plan, the coach, in league with the pastor, will envision the future training track.

The care system involves coaching the leaders. Cell churches believe that each cell leader needs a coach. Some cell churches set leaders over geographical districts, zones and areas of the city. Others supervised their leaders through homogenous departments. The coach will write in the action plan the care structure to be used in the future.

Budget

"Put your money where your mouth is." This well-used saying applies to your cell church. If you're a cell church or transitioning to become one, your budget should reflect this reality. The budget of the church should reflect what's important to the church. If cell church is the base, the backbone, it will show in the budget. Thus, in the stage of envisioning the future of the church, the pastor envisions what he'll need to spend on cell material and resources.

Faith Goals for New Cell Group

One of the key goals of cell churches is the number of cell groups at the end of the year. The goal of new cells is really a goal of how many new leaders are being equipped and sent out as harvest workers. The cell strategy focuses on raising up laborers as the key way to reach the rest of the world. Cell ministry concentrates on raising up disciples who will raise up disciples and then reach the world. Dale Galloway wrote, "The concept is that first you build leaders. The leaders build groups. Out of these groups come more leaders and a multiplication into more groups." [60]

The year goal is the most concrete, workable goal. A one-year goal demands immediate work. It can't be put off to another day. It must be dealt with right now. You will determine the yearly cell goal as you work with the pastor to find out the state of the current cells, how the training track is functioning and whether leaders are cared for. The general health of the church must also be evaluated.

4. Fulfill the Action Plan: On-going Coaching

Once the action plan is complete, the coach's job is to help the coachee fulfill the objectives.

If the pastor desires to change the action plan or make his own plan, the coach is always ready to serve and place the pastor in the driver's seat. The pastor is in charge, not the coach. The coach is there to serve and assist the pastor's accomplishment of his plan. The coach simply comes alongside and helps the pastor get to that desired haven.

I coached one church that was fully committed to a particular action plan. Both the lead pastor and the cell champion were running with the vision, but then the pastor's wife became a major obstacle in the process, and we went through major adjustments. The fact is that not all action plans will come to pass. People move on, pastoral staff change churches, and some pastors realize that their goals were too big. Some pastors have to first deal with personal struggles, such as a family crisis. Remember that primary role as coach is to serve the pastor, not to fulfill the action plan.

Toward the end of the coaching time with the pastor, I will do more nitty-gritty consulting and fine-tuning. At this time, the time table is ticking away. The finish line is near. The end is in sight. The coaching process may become more intense as we approach the agreed upon finish time.

5. Coaching someone else

If coaching is to become a movement, it must not stop with one generation of coaching. It must be passed on from coach to coachee, so that the coachee becomes the coach of new leaders.

I coached Jeff Tunnell and his pastoral team. Jeff was definitely a FAT coachee: faithful, available, teachable. He listened well, asked questions, and practiced what he learned in our coaching time. Toward the end of our coaching time together, I recommended Jeff to another pastor, needing help on his cell journey. And just like I thought, Jeff turned out to be an excellent coach.

When a pastor gives out, he learns so much more. This is one of the key benefits behind coaching someone else. When a person disperses knowledge, more is gained. Knowledge left to itself becomes like stagnant water. It's like the Dead Sea with nowhere to go. Coaching benefits the coach. The coachee will learn so much more when he or she can coach someone else.

You Can Coach

We entitled this book *You Can Coach* because we believe it's true. You can coach. Coaching doesn't require a higher degree, special talent, unique personality, or particular spiritual gift.

We believe, in fact, that God wants coaching to become a movement. We long to see the day in which every pastor has a coach and in turn is coaching someone else.

We believe that simple, timeless principles make the best foundation for coaching pastors. We've tried to share with you what we've learned. Now it's time for response.

Often the hardest part is taking that first step and expressing your willingness to coach someone else. We encourage you to take that first step, contact that pastor, or make yourself available to your leader. Do what it takes to apply the concepts in this book while they are fresh in your mind. As you depend on God to work through you as you coach, He will give you wisdom and insight like you never dreamed, and He will make you a great coach in the process.

Comiskey's Coaching Evaluation

I ask the pastors I'm coaching to evaluate me four times per year. I rotate between oral, personal evaluations, and anonymous ones. Thus, a year cycle for a group of pastors I'm coaching would look like this:

- End of March: oral/personal evaluations
- End of June: anonymous evaluations
- End of September: oral/personal evaluations
- End of December: anonymous evaluations

Oral/Personal Evaluation

During the personal evaluations, I'll ask each pastor individually what he or she thinks of my coaching. I'll ask him or her to give me suggestions and feedbacks. I don't use a particular form because it's more of a spontaneous interview. I just listen and write down what the coachee says. This information is invaluable, and it helps me to improve my coaching.

Anonymous Evaluation

I will send these evaluations out via email attachments and tell each pastor to complete it without his or her name. I then ask the coachee to return the completed evaluation to a secretary, administrator, or friend (someone besides myself). This "administrative" person will receive the evaluations and then send me a summary of what the coachees have written. I think the process works best via email, but you may prefer to have the coachees send it via regular postal mail.

The reason I use anonymous evaluations is because sometimes the coachee might not share everything in a personal interview. Some coachees are more free to share how they feel under the cover of anonymity.

Since my goal is to improve my coaching, I want to make sure I receive all the suggestions the coachees have to offer.

The Form I Use for the Anonymous Evaluations

You'll have to adapt this form to your own situation. For example, not all of the pastors I coach come to my house for coaching. Thus, I'll send out a slightly adapted form to those who don't come to my house.

I want strive to offer effective coaching. You can help me by providing comments and feedback. Please complete the following questions and send them back to me. Your feedback will be used to help me to prepare for our next meeting.

Date _____

	Excellent	Very Good	Good	Adequate	Poor
1. Please rate the over-all coaching experience	5	4	3	2	1
• Comment					
2. Rate the phone call time (s)	5	4	3	2	1
• Comment					
3. Rate the email contact	5	4	3	2	1
• Comment					

4. Please list the most useful skills, techniques or information you learned.

5. What recommendation do you have to make my coaching more effective? (please use the back, if necessary)

TELL ME MORE!

If you would like to share any feedback, or offer any comments, please do so on the back

Ben Wong's Coaching Agreement

Overriding Principles

1. No control and no glory – the purpose is not to control the church to be coached. The role is only to serve, and the relationship must be based on honor and not control. Helping another church does NOT convey any authority or control to the church which gives the help. The church being helped does not come under the control or supervision of the helping church. No one should get the glory except God Himself.

2. This is a part of the ministry of CCMN. We are a cell church network so we are coaching churches to become cell-based. When we say cell-based, we do not have a picture of how many cells so a house church could be a cell church. We are not talking about a mega-church.

3. The relationship is based on love and concern for the church being developed. The church giving the help does NOT expect anything in return. Helping another is an act of giving, an act of love in Jesus' name. Nothing is expected in return. The only obligations are:
   a. Be grateful for the help.
   b. Be eager and willing to help another church in need in the future.

4. The relationship is based on the full consent of both parties. Even though you need the help, I cannot help you unless you recognize

your situation and agree to receive help. Both parties must actively and wholeheartedly participate if the partnership is to be successful.

5. The church being coached must be willing and ready to change. This change may involve not only the way we do things, but the life of the leaders, especially the life of the pastor.

6. There is to be no financial obligations for all parties--no financial obligation to support the church to be coached. And the church to be coached does not have any financial obligation to finance any of the visits by the mentoring church. The relationship is fully voluntary, and the mentoring church should be ready to bear the cost of travel and accommodation.

Any financial transaction is to be on a fully voluntary basis. The church to be coached may want to give something towards the mentoring church's expenses if he feels led by God to do so, but must not feel obligated.

If we base this whole relationship on the servant heart of Jesus, then we could make everything very simple – food and accommodation – and avoid spending too much money out of the desire to be hospitable, which is a Japanese custom.

Basic Proposals
(What does the Coaching Relationship Involve?)

1. The initial coaching commitment is for one year and will not be longer than three years.

2. The coaching is to help develop an indigenous Cell Model for the local church (the mentoring church model can be an example to glean from, but we must not impose a model to the local church, but rather help the local church to find its own model).

3. The Key is Life – the life is what will bring growth. Help develop a life building model, including "running life changing camps," building discipling relationships, and structures into the church

(accountability and building up of life), building important atmospheres in the church, etc. Much of this will involve the change of life of the leaders, especially the pastor.

4. Instilling (or infusion of) new life into the pastor, helping him see that his life can be different. This will include: maintaining the fire, living by faith in God, being courageous and bold, becoming more a fighter for God rather than a scholar mentality that has been formed by the seminary, living in inspiration rather than institution, being close to the members of the church, building relationships, being more fun, etc. Most pastors are introverted because they are used to the seminary model of preparing things in the office. Jesus' ministry is more outside than in the building. Jesus trained people outside and not inside the building. Help the pastor to be a pastor of the city rather than in the city.

5. Extraordinary prayer for the church to be coached. This should involve intense focused prayer. This prayer must be based on specific needs, so the local church needs to be diligent in communicating its needs to the mentoring church.

6. Mobilization of workers: brothers and sisters from the mentoring church could be mobilized to make mission trips to the church being coached to make strategic breakthroughs for the church. This could be in the form of waves of short-term teams working together with local brothers and sisters. Teams could come to help with training, evangelisms, camps, etc. One whole church helping another whole church.

7. Coaching commitment: Ben will aim to come four times in the first year, and the mentoring church should aim to meet the church to be coached at least two times a month for relationship building, coaching, and helping.

8. The church to be coached can visit the mentoring church in order to be exposed to how they are doing it, and glean ideas, and catch the life of the church there.

9. The churches should be committed to regularly networking with other healthy cell churches in Kansai so they can learn from each other and together do the ministry of the Kingdom.

10. The Church to be coached should plan to help other needy churches in the same region. Reproduction is the requirement.

Index

A

active listening   37, 40, 52
adaptable structure   127
Alan Hirsh   121
Albania   17, 31
Anna   25, 69, 70, 88
Anonymous Evaluations   12, 140
Ara Parseghian   98
art   6, 7, 55
Asia   3, 17, 56

B

Ben Wong   1, 6, 7, 9, 10, 11, 12,
        16, 17, 18, 21, 46, 59, 81,
        107, 143, 145, 152, 153
Bob Moffitt   4

C

case study   53, 131, 132
Catherine   25, 69, 70, 88
CCMN   53, 143
cell churches   84, 109, 135, 136,
        146, 148, 154
Cell Church Mission Network   16
cell group   75, 110, 134
cell ministry   5, 77, 130, 131, 132
China   16, 152
Christian Schwarz   118, 153, 154
Chubu   84
church planting   71, 100, 134, 154

Coaching Group   9, 28
coaching network   17, 61, 62,
        63, 64, 65, 67, 68, 71, 83,
        84, 85, 86, 87, 88, 89, 90,
        91, 116, 117, 119, 125, 153
Comiskey   1, 2, 3, 4, 6, 9, 10, 11,
        12, 16, 17, 18, 49, 55, 73,
        129, 139, 141, 148, 152,
        153, 155
commitment   60, 64, 65, 78, 83,
        129, 144, 145
confidentiality   77
confront   50, 52
counseling   18, 57, 82

D

Dale Galloway   136, 155
Darrow L. Miller   4
David Yonggi Cho   75
DISC   35, 36, 132
disciplines   34, 35, 54
dream   4, 18, 19, 21, 26, 30, 31,
        33, 34, 35, 37, 38, 39, 41,
        42, 43, 44, 45, 46, 87, 89,
        93, 94, 97, 98, 99, 100, 101,
        102, 103, 126, 133
Dream-based Coaching   9, 31,
        45, 101
DreamWeaver   17, 31

E

East Asian   61, 62, 154
Eiichi Hamasaki   5
encouragement   4, 13, 34, 36,
      52, 54, 66, 67, 78, 82, 85,
      90, 103
encouraging   28, 49, 50
Eric Watt   5
essences   61, 67, 109, 111, 114,
      123, 127, 154
evaluate   19, 28, 52, 111, 139
evaluation   58, 65, 139

F

failure   60, 64, 65, 78, 83, 129,
      144, 145
family   7, 8, 24, 28, 29, 45, 53,
      62, 63, 64, 66, 69, 70, 74,
      75, 79, 86, 88, 93, 113, 115,
      116, 132, 137, 154
Federer   51
feedback   50, 58
friendship   5, 51, 73, 74, 75, 76,
      77, 79
Friendship-based Coaching   10,
      73, 153

G

Gary Collins   82
gift mix   35, 36
giving   6, 18, 27, 32, 36, 39, 45,
      49, 51, 55, 56, 57, 71, 82,
      101, 104, 115, 125, 143
God-dreams   31, 33, 34, 35, 41, 42,
      43, 45, 46, 93, 98, 99, 100,
      101, 103

Greg Popovich   75
Group Evangelism   93

H

Hong Kong   4, 6, 7, 10, 16, 17,
      18, 21, 22, 24, 27, 46, 53,
      68, 88, 115, 125, 152
house churches   109

I

Indonesia   21, 108, 111, 152
influence   19, 43, 59, 87, 98, 99,
      100, 101, 104

J

Japan   5, 7, 16, 64, 71, 83, 84,
      85, 86, 87, 90, 91, 115, 116,
      117, 126, 153
Jean-Marc Terrel   6
Joel Comiskey   1, 2, 3, 6, 9, 10,
      11, 16, 17, 18, 49, 55, 73,
      129, 148, 152, 153, 155
Joel Comiskey Group   2
joelcomiskeygroup.com   1, 2
John Wooden   15
Joseph Umidi   3, 102

K

Kansai   83, 84, 85, 86, 146, 153
Kanto   84, 85, 153
Karen Hurston   75
Kevin Wood   57
Korea   16, 70, 148

L

Larry Kreider   6
leadership development   3, 35,

133, 147

Leadership Explosion   135

learning   16, 34, 55, 57, 59, 83, 108, 129

Lifeforming Leadership Coaching   3, 35, 102, 105

listen   4, 16, 17, 36, 37, 38, 41, 50, 51, 53, 54, 60, 96, 100, 101, 122, 139

listening   18, 26, 30, 37, 38, 40, 41, 49, 50, 51, 52, 53, 54, 55, 57, 101

lonely pastors   21, 30, 34, 87, 89

LRQ Cycle   101

M

Malaysia   23

Malcolm   68

marriage   8, 62, 63, 65, 66, 69, 102, 116, 132

Master Coach   32, 37, 45, 95, 96, 97

John Maxwell   44, 66, 152

mega-churches   60, 70, 71, 110

mentoring   4, 23, 68, 101, 144, 145

Michael Frost   121, 155

Michael Mackerell   4

missionary   5, 17, 24, 26, 57

Mobilization   145

models   5, 95, 102, 107, 108, 109, 127

Moreno Valley   2

multiplication   71, 118, 135, 136

N

Navigators   22

network   17, 18, 27, 28, 60, 61, 62, 63, 64, 65, 67, 68, 71, 83, 84, 85, 86, 87, 88, 89, 90, 91, 116, 117, 119, 125, 143, 153

New Testament   60, 108, 112, 114, 116, 123

North America   16, 148

O

open questions   38, 39, 40

oral evaluation   58

ordinary pastors   81, 87, 89, 91

Øystein Gjerme   5

P

passion   3, 4, 19, 26, 46, 65

personality   35, 36, 51, 53, 58, 63, 132, 138, 155

personality profile   36

pitfalls   42, 93, 94, 104

Planting Churches that Reproduce   134

positive affirmation   41

powerful questions   18, 32, 34, 39, 40, 41, 46, 49, 50, 96

principles   3, 4, 5, 6, 15, 16, 17, 19, 32, 44, 49, 54, 59, 73, 83, 108, 109, 111, 130, 135, 138, 153, 154

Q

questions   4, 17, 18, 32, 34, 36, 37, 38, 39, 40, 41, 44, 46, 49, 50, 52, 53, 54, 57, 73, 96, 100, 101, 108, 131, 137

R

Ralph W. Neighbour, Jr   3
Reinhard Bonnke   100
relationship   18, 29, 32, 33, 36,
          37, 38, 39, 40, 55, 60, 62,
          63, 64, 65, 67, 74, 75, 76,
          79, 85, 90, 93, 104, 111,
          112, 113, 114, 116, 118,
          123, 143, 144, 145
relationships   6, 8, 16, 22, 62,
          63, 64, 66, 75, 99, 111, 113,
          114, 127, 144, 145, 153,
          154
Reproduction   146
resources   18, 67, 68, 107, 120,
          136
Robert Clinton   63, 152
Robert Michael Lay   7

S

President Sali Berisha   31
Sam   1, 4, 5, 6, 7, 17, 18, 19
Sam Scaggs   1, 6, 17, 18
Scaggs   1, 4, 6, 9, 11, 17, 18, 31,
          93
servant   34, 45, 54, 73, 130, 144
Servanthood   52, 54
serving   5, 17, 32, 43, 59, 88, 97,
          114
Shepherd Community
          Church   4, 18, 125
Shikoku   84, 86, 91, 119
small churches   25, 61, 70, 71,
          110
statistics   30, 77
Stephen Covey   78
Strength Finder   132

Stuart Gramenz   6
Sunny Cheng   6

T

Taiwan   7, 16, 152
teaching   18, 32, 36, 37, 50, 52,
          53, 55, 57, 74, 76, 101, 120,
          121, 123, 134, 152
Timothy Tu   8
Tony and Felicity Dale   3
Tony Chan   4
toolbox   18, 19, 50, 54
tools   4, 6, 18, 19, 32, 33, 47, 58,
          104
Touch   16, 17, 155
traditional churches   109
training   3, 17, 18, 21, 27, 28, 33,
          44, 50, 52, 59, 74, 75, 81,
          82, 83, 93, 94, 97, 102, 104,
          105, 107, 119, 120, 130,
          134, 135, 136, 145
transformation   32, 33, 93, 95,
          103, 104
transition   33, 88, 133, 134

U

unity   27, 112, 113, 114, 118

V

vulnerable   55

W

Wayne Cordeiro   31, 34, 35
William Moulton Marston   35
Wolfgang Simson   7
Wong   1, 4, 6, 7, 9, 10, 11, 12,
          16, 17, 18, 21, 46, 59, 81,

Endnotes

Chapter 1: Everyone Needs a Coach by Ben Wong

1. N There was severe persecution of Chinese in Indonesia at that time, and my parents sent all the children out of the country. We scattered all around the world – Australia, Taiwan, and USA – but I chose to go back to Hong Kong.

2. Beginning in 1966, there was the Cultural Revolution in China, and life was very tough for many people in China. Hong Kong was also affected and there were open riots in the streets. My parents were anxious, and so they sent me away from Hong Kong.

3. This is not her real name. The stories have been changed so that the real person is represented but not to be recognized.

4. Subsequently I have discovered that there are some people who are coaching others and teaching others to coach. Bob Logan and the ChurchSmart Team have developed some good materials on this.

5. Pastoral Care Inc, 2009

Chapter 3: The Coaching Toolbox by Joel Comiskey

6. At the time, a particular denomination paid half of my salary, and each individual church had to pay a portion as well. I received most of my income this way.

7. http://sports.espn.go.com/sports/tennis/wimbledon08/columns/story?columnist=harwitt_sandra&id=3473761

8. I keep a running record of my leaders in order to stay up-to-date with them and to pray more effectively. My file for each of my leaders has grown tremendously. I use this information as prayer fodder. I pray over the leader's weakness and pinpoint strengths in the midst of all the weakness.

Chapter 4: Principles We Have Learned in Coaching by Ben Wong

9. This is a term that we will use for the person being coached.

10. Philippians 4:8 (The Message)

11. Dr. J. Robert Clinton, Finishing Well, 1999

12. Jeremiah 17:9

13. This is a Chinese proverb.

14. John Maxwell, Encouragement Changes Everything: Bless and be Blessed.

15. Colossians 1:28-29

16. James 1:5

Chapter 5: Friendship-based Coaching by Joel Comiskey

17. Jay Firebaugh, It all comes down to relationships (Houston, TX: The Coach is the Key, 1999), p. 41.

18. As quoted in "Quietly, Popovich is becoming one of the greats." Accessed in June 2007 from http://www.usatoday.com/sports/basketball/nba/spurs/2007-06-13-popovich_N.htm

19. David B. Peterson and Mary Dee Hicks, Leader as Coach: Strategies for Coaching and Developing Others (Minneapolis, MN: Personnel Decisions International, 1996), p. 43.

20. Gary R. Collins, How to be a People Helper (Wheaton, IL: Tyndale House Publishers, 1995).

Chapter 6: Ordinary Pastors Can Coach by Ben Wong

21. When Jesus was asked who is my neighbor, He answered with the Parable of the Good Samaritan, which tells us that our neighbor is not the person who lives next door but someone in need who cannot help himself (Luke 10:29-37).

22. Gary R. Collins, How to be a People Helper , preface.

23. I got the idea from being with Robert Lay in Brazil. He has been running ACT (Advance Cell Training), a course on the Cell Church, all over Brazil. It is a mini-seminar that occurs four times per year and lasts for three days. These gatherings enable the students to be consistently reinforced in the key teachings and also interact with others. In between the seminars, the students need to practice what is being taught.

24. There are a few famous cities in Kansai area, such as Osaka, Kyoto and Kobe.

25. I do not charge anything for my part in the coaching network because many of the churches that need coaching are very small and the burden of having to pay a fee will be a great deterrent for them to join. Also, the atmosphere that we want to set is that you do not need to pay back anything for the coaching you receive – but pay it forward.

26. This agreement is in the Appendix for you to look at. We modified this agreement for each place so that it is culturally sensitive. Again, most churches that need help are very small and are under financial burden. The coaches are pastors of churches and so they already have support from their church, so they can offer their coaching free of charge. If the coachee wants to give an offering, then the coach is also free to receive it.

27. Since we were just starting with Kanto Coaching Network, we were still quite conservative and not sure that such an ordinary pastor could coach.

28. In Japan, on an average, a church does not have even one baptism per year!

Chapter 8: Coaching by Focusing on the Essence by Ben Wong

29. Christian Schwarz in his book, Natural Church Development, has outlined eight Universal Principles, which he has discovered through researching 1000 churches in 32 countries. These principles are very interesting and are the basis of the survey that a church can do to discover which of these principles the church

is strong in and which it is weak in. The result is used by coaches to help build healthier churches (ChurchSmart Resources).

30. This was precipitated by the appearance of the G12 model that came out of Bogota, Columbia. They brought quite a lot of controversy by calling people to exactly follow their model. Also at this time, the "House Church" model was being introduced to us. In one of their very representing book, "Houses that changed the World," the author used one chapter to criticize the cell churches. This brought some polarity into the pastors at the summit.

31. 1 Corinthians 3:4

32. Even if you do not agree with these Seven Essences, you should be focusing on the principles and not the model when it comes to coaching pastors.

33. Most of the Asian cultures, especially the East Asians, are performance-oriented cultures. We grow up with parents measuring whether we are a good child by our performances in school. Pleasing your parents means that you have to work hard in performing well in all areas of your life – in school, in playing the piano, in sport, in front of the relatives, etc. So when we are adults, we still have this performance complex, and we pass it on to our next generation.

34. If you are interested in these essences, be on the lookout for a book that will come out where I will write in details these 7 essences and how they apply to the church.

35. This is the Greek word for "church."

36. Ephesians 2:19

37. Ephesians 2:21

38. Ephesians 2:22

39. Ephesians 5:22-33

40. Ephesians 6:1-4

41. Ephesians 6:5-9

42. Many Asian cultures--and definitely with the East Asian (Chinese, Japanese and Koreans) cultures – outsiders are treated better than our closest family relations. In fact, we treat the people closest to us the worst. That is why coaching pastors in building good relationships with their spouse, children and lay leadership in the church is very important.

43. Luke 9:23-24

44. Acts 20:35 (Message)

45. John 20:21

46. By this we mean the church of a coach.

47. They are launching this vision in October, 2010, but they already have more than ten groups ready to start a new church. They are just waiting for the church to officially launch this church planting.

48. Natural Church Development, Christian Schwarz, p. 22-23.

49. Ephesians 4:11-12 (Amplified)

50. Matthew 5:3 (Message)

51. John 16:33 (Message)

52. James 1:2-4 (Message)

53.   Michael Frost and Alan Hirsch, ReJesus: A Wild Messiah for a Missional Church, Introduction

54.   Luke 19:10

55.   This is unheard of in a Korean church. They always are formal and wear a suit and tie.

Chapter 9: Making a Coaching Plan by Joel Comiskey

56.   Interview with Peter Wagner, Strategies for Today's Leaders (third quarter, 2002), p. 8.

57.   ProScan is an excellent analysis of personality, whether the leader is in the right environment and satisfaction levels. stress levels. For more information, contact Debra Schottelkorb at viewthrulight@verizon.net

58.   William A. Beckham, The Second Reformation (Houston, TX: Touch Publications, 1995), p. 168.

59.   Dale Galloway started his small-group church by forming the initial group which he led in his home. Out of that initial group he trained leaders for the next groups who passed on the vision to new leadership. Even Jesus started by forming His own prototype cell. He spent years developing the model. He couldn't afford failure. David Cho founded the largest church in the history of Christianity, but he counsels new cell church pastors to start small: "Take a dozen key lay leaders and train them as cell leaders. Then have them form their own home cell meetings, and watch over them carefully for six to eight months. Once this group of cells has begun to bear fruit, it will be time to get the whole church involved."

60.   Dale Galloway, 20-20 Vision (Portland, OR: Scott Publishing House, 1986), p. 155.